# REPRESENTATION AND RETRIEVAL OF VISUAL MEDIA IN MULTIMEDIA SYSTEMS

*edited by*


**HongJiang Zhang**
*Hewlett Packard Laboratories*

**Philippe Aigrain**
*Universite Paul Sabatier*

**Dragutin Petkovic**
*IBM Almaden Research Center*



*A Special Issue of*
**MULTIMEDIA TOOLS AND APPLICATIONS**
**An International Journal**
**Volume 3, No. 3 (1996)**

SPRINGER SCIENCE+BUSINESS MEDIA, LLC

# MULTIMEDIA TOOLS AND APPLICATIONS

## An International Journal

Volume 3, No. 3, November 1996

***Special Issue on Representation and Retrieval of Visual Media in Multimedia Systems***
***Guest Editors: HongJiang Zhang, Philippe Aigrain, and Dragutin Petkovic***

ISBN 978-1-4757-8279-0 ISBN 978-0-585-34549-9 (eBook)
DOI 10.1007/978-0-585-34549-9

**Library of Congress Cataloging-in-Publication Data**

A C.I.P. Catalogue record for this book is available
from the Library of Congress.


Originally published by Kluwer Academic Publishers in 1996
Softcover reprint of the hardcover 1st edition 1996



*Printed on acid-free paper.*

Multimedia Tools and Applications 3, 177–178 (1996)


# Introduction to Special Issue on Representation and Retrieval of Visual Media in Multimedia Systems

With rapid advances in communication and multimedia computing technologies, accessing mass amounts of multimedia data is becoming a reality on the Information Superhighway and in digital libraries. However, interacting with multimedia data, images and video in particular, is not merely a matter of connecting everyone with data banks and delivering data via networks to everyone's home and office. It is definitely not enough simply to store and display images and video as in commercial video-on-demand services. What we need are new technologies for parsing and representing the content of visual data to facilitate organization, storage, query and retrieval of mass collections of image and video data in a user-friendly way. This need poses many research challenges to scientists and engineers across all multimedia computing disciplines. Important issues identified by researchers include:

- Effective feature-based pattern analysis and content representation for visual data classification, browsing, retrieval, filtering and compression.
- Perceptual similarity measures based on object color, texture and shape; effective and efficient indexing schemes based on these features; and their evaluations based on large collections of data.
- Automatic parsing and classification of video data; video content representation, especially for supporting "event-based" retrieval.
- Automatic/semiautomatic annotation of images and video based on visual features, to support text based retrieval of visual media.
- Automatic/semiautomatic abstraction of video content in both visual media and non-visual media, such as text.
- Image and video analysis, classification, and retrieval based on compressed data.
- Fusion of information derived from different media, especially sound/speech/music and close captions, for video content parsing.
- Integration of content-based retrieval with traditional database technologies in applications.
- Data modeling of visual media in multimedia databases and information systems.
- Visual tools and interfaces for query formation, visual feedback, presentation of retrieval results, and content-based browsing of visual media.
- Application systems which embody state-of-the-art techniques in visual media archival and retrieval.

This special issue of Multimedia Tools and Applications is devoted to these research topics, with the emphasis on implemented prototypes, tools and applications and will be published as two issues due to the large number of high quality submissions. This first issue include four papers and four more papers will be published in the following issue. The first paper by the guest editors presents a comprehensive survey of the state-of-the-art techniques, algorithms and tools in content-based analysis and representation of visual media, and their application to the abstracting, indexing, retrieval, browsing, interactive perception, annotation and re-use of visual data. The paper by Cha and Lee described a novel iconic browser for multimedia databases, which allows effective and simultaneous browsing and navigating of multimedia objects, especially visual objects. The paper by Zhang, Biao and Acharya addresses the problem of image indexing and retrieval using fractal representation of the compressed images directly and presented an effective solution for indexing and searching of similar images. Finally, the paper by Wu and his colleagues reports their work in developing a multimedia trademark registration system and provides insights on several key issues on applying content-based image indexing and retrieval techniques in real application systems, including: feature extraction, multiple feature fusion, similarity measures, and integrating of content-based methods with traditional database methods.

We believe that, though it is impossible to cover all the research topics in one special issue, the four papers presented here reflect the state of the art of the field. We hope this special issue will attract more researchers and thus contribute to the field.

Guest editors:
**HongJiang Zhang**
**Philippe Aigrain**
**Dragutin Petkovic**

Multimedia Tools and Applications 3, 179–202 (1996)


# Content-Based Representation and Retrieval of Visual Media: A State-of-the-Art Review

PHILIPPE AIGRAIN
*Institut de Recherche en Informatique de Toulouse, Université Paul Sabatier, 118, route de Narbonne, F-31062 Toulouse Cedex, France*

HONGJIANG ZHANG[1]
*Broadband Information Systems Lab., Hewlett-Packard Labs., 1501 Page Mill Road, Palo Alto, CA94304, USA*

DRAGUTIN PETKOVIC
*IBM Almaden Research Center, San Jose, CA 95120-6099, USA*

**Abstract.** This paper reviews a number of recently available techniques in content analysis of visual media and their application to the indexing, retrieval, abstracting, relevance assessment, interactive perception, annotation and re-use of visual documents.

**Keywords:** content-based retrieval, image, video, texture, colour, editing, shot, sequence, indexing, visual interfaces, soundtrack, video browsers

## 1. Background

A few years ago, the problems of representation and retrieval of visual media were confined to specialized image databases (geographical, medical, pilot experiments in computerized slide libraries), in the professional applications of the audiovisual industries (production, broadcasting and archives), and in computerized training or education. The present development of multimedia technology and information highways has put content processing of visual media at the core of key application domains: digital and interactive video, large distributed digital libraries, multimedia publishing. Though the most important investments have been targeted at the information infrastructure (networks, servers, coding and compression, delivery models, multimedia systems architecture), a growing number of researchers have realized that content processing will be a key asset in putting together successful applications. The need for content processing techniques has been made evident from a variety of angles, ranging from achieving better quality in compression, allowing user choice of programs in video-on-demand, achieving better productivity in video production, providing access to large still image databases or integrating still images and video in multimedia publishing and cooperative work.

Content-based retrieval of visual media and representation of visual documents in human-computer interfaces are based on the availability of content representation data (time-structure for time-based media, image signatures, object and motion data). When it is possible, the human production of this descriptive data is so time consuming—and thus costly—that it is almost impossible to generate it for large document spaces. There is some hope that for video documents, some of this data will be created at production time and coded in the document itself. Nonetheless it will never be available for many existing documents, and when considering the history of media and carriers one is lead to a very cautious estimate of how often this type of information will be really available even in future documents. Thus, there is a clear need for automatic analysis tools which are able to extract representation data from the documents.

The researchers involved in content processing efforts come from various backgrounds, for instance:

- the publishing, entertainment, retail or document industry where researchers try to extend their activity to visual documents, or to integrate them in hypertext-based new document types,
- the AV hardware and software industry, primarily interested by digital editing tools and other programma production tools,
- academic and national research laboratories where research had been conducted for some time on computer analysis and access to existing visual media, such as the MIT Media Laboratory [48], the Institute of System Sciences in Singapore [71], or IRIT in France [3].
- large telecommunication company laboratories, where researchers are primarily interesting in cooperative work and remote access to visual media,
- the robotics vision, signal processing, image sequence processing for security, or data compression research communities who try to find new applications for their models of images or human perception.
- computer companies developing digital library, multimedia databases and other multimedia applications or home appliances, such as IBM Almaden Research Center [23], NTT [61], Hitachi [63], Siemens Research [14] and Virage.

These researchers originally used very different models and techniques and often conflicting vocabulary. After a few years of lively confusion and exciting achievements, it is now possible to draw a clearer panorama of the state of this emerging field, and to outline some of its possible directions of development.

In this paper, we review the methods available for different types of visual content analysis, representation and their application and survey some open research problems. Section 2 covers various visual features for representing and comparing image content. Sections 3 reviews video content parsing and representation algorithms and schemes, including temporal segmentation, video abstraction, shot comparison and soundtrack analysis. Section 4 presents applications of visual representation schemes in content-based image and video retrieval and browsing. Finally, Section 5 summaries our survey and current research directions.

## 2. The many facets of image similarity

Retrieval of still images by similarity, i.e., retrieving images which are similar to an already retrieved image (retrieval by example) or to a model or schema is a relatively old idea. Some might date it to the mnemotechnical ideas of the antiquity, but more seriously it appeared in specialized geographical information systems databases around 1980, in particular in the Query by Pictorial Example system of IMAID [19]. From the start, it was clear that retrieval by similarity called for specific definitions of what it means to be similar. In the mapping system, a satellite image was matched to existing map images from the point of view of similarity of road and river networks, easily extracted from images by edge detection. Apart from paper models [2, 8], it was only in the beginning of the 90s that researchers started to look at retrieval by similarity in large set of heterogeneous images with no specific model of their semantic contents. The prototype systems of Kato [38], followed by the availability of the QBIC commercial system using several types of similarities [23] contributed to making this idea more and more popular.

A system for retrieval by similarity rests on 3 components:

- extraction of features or image signatures from the images, and an efficient representation and storage strategy for this precomputed data,
- a set of similarity measures, each of which captures some perceptively meaningful definition of similarity, and which should be efficiently computable when matching an example with the whole database,
- a user interface for the choice of which definition(s) of similarity should be applied for retrieval, and for the ordered and visually efficient presentation of retrieved images and for supporting relevance feedback.

Recent work has made evident that:

- A large number of meaningful types of similarity can and must be defined. Only part of these definitions are associated with efficient feature extraction mechanisms and (dis)similarity measures.
- Since there are many definitions of similarity and the discriminating power of each of the measures is likely to degrade significantly for large image databases, the user interface and the feature storage strategy components of the systems will play a more and more essential role. We will come back to this point in Section 4.1.
- Visual content based retrieval is best utilized when combined with the traditional search, both at user interface and the system level. The basic reason for this is that we do not see the possibility of content based retrieval replacing the ability of parametric (SQL) search, text and keywords to represent the rich semantic content of the visual material (names, places, action, prices, etc.). The key is to apply content based retrieval where appropriate, and this is where the use of text and keywords is suboptimal. Examples of such applications are where visual appearance (e.g., color, texture, shape, motion) are important search arguments like in stock photo/video, art, retail, on-line shopping etc. Not only content based retrieval reduces the high variability among human indexers, but it also enables more "fuzzy" browsing and search which in many application is an essential part of the process. It is obvious then that content based retrieval involves strong user interaction, thus necessitating the development of special fast browsers and UI techniques.

In this section we briefly survey the various types of similarity definitions and associated feature extraction and measures for systems which do not assume any specific image domain or a-priori semantic knowledge on the images.

Gudivada has listed possible types of similarity for retrieval in [26]: color similarity, texture similarity, shape similarity, spatial similarity, etc. Some of these types can be considered in all or only part of one image, can be considered independently of scale or angle or not, depending on whether one is interested in the scene represented by the image or in the image per se.

### 2.1. *Color similarity*

Color distribution similarity has been one of the first choices [23, 33] because if one chooses a proper representation and measure it can be partially reliable even in presence of changes in lighting, view angle, and scale. For the capture of properties of the global color distribution in images, the need for a perceptively meaningful color model leads to the choice of HLS (Hue-Luminosity-Saturation) models, and of measures based on the 3 first moments of color distributions [57] preferably to histogram distances. It has been proposed in [11] to use hue and saturation distributions only when one wants to capture lighting-independent color distribution properties which are good signatures of a scene when the scale does not change too much. In this case one can identify the hue-saturation perceptive space with the complex unit discuss and define measures using statistical moments in this space. This is useful to avoid biases of measures which do not take in account the circular nature of hue, and could be further refined to distinguish between true spectral hues and the purples. Stricker and Orengo have argued in [57] for the importance of including the 3rd moment (distribution skewness) in the definition of the similarity measure.

One important difficulty with color similarity is that when using it for retrieval, an user will often be looking for an image "with a red object such as this one". This problem of restricting color similarity to a spatial component, and more generally of combining spatial similarity and color similarity is also present for texture similarity. It explains why prototype and commercial systems have included complex ad-hoc mechanisms in their user interfaces to combine various similarity functions.

### 2.2. *Texture similarity*

For texture as for color, it is essential to define a well-funded perceptive space. Picard and Liu [49] have shown that it is possible to do so using the Wold decomposition of the texture considered as a luminance field. One gets three components (periodic, evanescent and random) corresponding to the bi-dimensional periodicity, mono-dimensional orientation, and complexity of the analyzed texture. Experiments have shown that these independent components agree well with the perceptive evaluation of texture similarity [59]. The related similarity measures has lead to remarkably efficient results including for the retrieval of large-scale textures such as images of buildings and cars [47]. In QBIC system, Tomura texture features, contrast, compactness and direction, are used [23]. But of course one is again confronted to the problem of combining texture information with the spatial organization of several textures (see below).

### 2.3. *Shape similarity*

A proper definition of shape similarity calls for the distinction between shape similarity in images (similarity between actual geometrical shapes appearing in the images) and shape similarity between the objects depicted by the images, i.e., similarity modulo a number of geometrical transformations corresponding to changes in view angle, optical parameters and scale. In some cases, one wants to include even deformation of non-rigid bodies. The first type of similarity has attracted research work only for calibrated image databases of special types of objects, such as ceramic plates. Even, in this case, the researchers have tried to define shape representations which are scale independent, resting on curvature, angle statistics and contour complexity. Systems such as QBIC [23] use circularity, eccentricity, major axis orientation (not angle-independent) and algebraic moment. It should be noted that in some cases the user of a retrieval system will want a definition of shape similarity which is dependent on view angle (for instance will want to retrieve trapezoids with an horizontal basis and not the other trapezoids).

In the general case, a promising approach has been proposed by Sclaroff and Pentland [53] in which shapes are represented as canonical deformations of prototype objects. In this approach, a "physical" model of the 2D-shape is built using a new form of Galerkin's interpolation method (finite-element discretization). The possible deformation modes are analyzed using Karhunen-Loeve transform. This yields an ordered list of deformation modes corresponding to rigid body modes (translation, rotation), low-frequency non-rigid modes associated to global deformations and higher-frequency modes associated to localized deformations.

As for color and texture, the present schemes for shape similarity modelling are faced with serious difficulties when images include several objects or background. A preliminary segmentation as well as modelling of spatial relationships between shapes is then necessary (are we interested in finding images where one region represents a shape similar to a given prototype or to some spatial organization of several shapes?).

### 2.4. *Spatial similarity*

Gudivada and Raghavan [27] have treated spatial similarity in the situation in which it is assumed that images have been (automatically or manually) segmented into meaningful objects, each object being associated with is centroid and a symbolic name. Such a representation is called a *symbolic image*, and it is relatively easy to define similarity functions for such image modulo transformations such as rotation, scaling and translation. Efforts have also been made to address spatial similarity directly (without segmentation and object indexing). This was the case, for instance, in the original work of Kato [38], in the limited case of direct spatial similarity (without geometrical transformation), using a number of ad-hoc statistical features computed on very low resolution images.

### 2.5. *Object presence analysis*

Finding images in which a particular object or type of object appears—all images with cars, all shots in a video in which a given character is present—is a particular case of similarity computation. Once again, the range of applicable methods is defined by the invariants of the object to be recognized. For color images, and for images whose color does not change, local color distribution is efficient, and can be reliable even when changes in scale or angle occur [45]. In the general case, the best results so far have been obtained with texture-based models [48]. A pyramidal analysis of texture (with the whole image considered as the texture and then spatial subblocks, etc.) has been shown to detect efficiently the local presence of objects at various scales. This is true not only for objects which we naturally think of as "texture-like" such as grass, water or clouds, but also for objects which are textured at much larger scale such as buildings or cars. When the problem is to locate images with a particular object (a particular face, a particular building) and not any object of a given type, principal component analysis methods of more general features of the images is the only efficient method. But, as we have seen in the previous section, their application to complex images of which the searched objects are only a part is still a largely open problem. It is worth to point out that object annotation by keywords is and will continue to be an efficient index for objects in images. But, more research is needed on algorithms that will assist human operators in generating these keywords.

### 2.6. *Summary*

In conclusion to this review of image similarity techniques, several main problems remain to be addressed for these techniques to be easily applicable to the full-range of access problems to large image databases:

- Study of the distribution of measures for various feature spaces on large real-world sets of images. In particular, how well is the perceived similarity order preserved by the measure when the number of images grows?
- Study of ranking visual items that correspond to human perception.
- Definition of methods for the segmentation of images in homogeneous regions for various feature spaces, and definition of models of this spatial organization which could be robustly combined with the similarity of the local features.
- Detection of salient features to a type of images or objects, so that to free user from specifying a particular set of features in query process.
- Combination of multiple visual features in image query and search.
- Developing efficient indexing schemes based on image similarity features for managing large databases. It has been shown that traditional database indexing techniques like R-trees, etc., fail in the context of content based image search, and currently there is no technique that allows retrieval of similar objects in multi-dimensional space. Ideas from statistical clustering, multi-dimensional indexing, and dimensionality reduction may be useful in this area.

Apart from these issues in extraction of low level visual features and establishment of related search/matching functions, extraction of higher (semantic) level image attributes (such as recognition of objects, human faces and actions) and related search/matching functions are definitely a more challenging task. Only when the features extracted at both these levels are combined, can content-based image indexes be built.

In addition, formalization of the whole paradigm of content based image retrieval to bring it to a sufficient level of consistency and integrity is essential to the success of the field. Without this formalism it will be hard to develop sufficiently reliable and mission critical applications that are easy to program and evaluate. Some early applications may be implemented without such a rigorous formalism, but the progress in the field will require full understanding of the basic requirements in content-based retrieval.

## 3. Video parsing and representation

To interact with video data is hard using conventional VCR-like video manipulation tools. The problem is that, from the point of view of content, the resources managed by the conventional systems are unstructured, apart from time code. Thus, the effort has been on introducing for structural and content analysis (parsing) of video, so that video can be indexed and accessed on the basis of structural properties and content.

Video parsing encompasses two tasks: temporal segmentation of a video program into elemental units, and content extraction from those units, based on both video and audio semantic primitives [71]. Many effective algorithms are now available for temporal segmentation. But, fully automated content extraction is a much more difficult task, requiring both signal analysis and knowledge representation techniques; so human assistance is still needed. On the other hand, the most fruitful research approach may be to concentrate on facilitating tools, using low-level visual features and content information from audio and close caption data. Such tools are clearly feasible and research in this direction should ultimately lead to an intelligent video retrieval and browsing systems [75].

In this section, we review a variety of video parsing and analysis approaches, including temporal segmentation of video, camera motion analysis, video soundtrack analysis, video abstraction approaches and shot similarity for shot comparison and clustering.

### *3.1. Temporal segmentation of video sequences*

A video shot can be defined as consecutive images which appear to have been continuously filmed. A collection of one or more adjoining shots that focus on an object or objects of interest may comprise a scene. Shots are obviously a fundamental unit of manipulation (production, indexing, representation) of video. Therefore, detecting shot boundaries has been one of the first issues address by many researchers in video content analysis, and many algorithms and schemes have been developed and published.

There are a number of different types of transitions or boundaries between shots. The simplest transition is a cut, an abrupt shot change which occurs between two consecutive frames. More sophisticated transitions include fades, dissolves and wipes, etc. A fade is a slow change in brightness of images usually resulting in or starting with a solid black frame. A dissolve occurs when the images of the first shot get dimmer and the images of the second shot get brighter, with frames within the transition showing one image superimposed on the other. A wipe occurs when pixels from the second shot replace those of the first shot in a regular pattern such as in a line from the right edge of the frames.

Some form of shot change detection was incorporated in the hardware of some telecine devices as early as the 1970's. Software researchers tried to address this problem from the beginning of the 1990's. The first researchers [44, 63] worked only on cut detection, which was natural for them since they were working in the frame of editing systems, and shot change detection was applied to unedited rushes. Later work [7, 56, 69, 70] has addressed shot change detection including the case of progressive transitions. The scientific problem of shot change detection consists in separating various factors of image change:

- Motion, including both camera work-induced apparent motion and object motion;
- Luminosity changes and noise;
- Shot change, abrupt or progressive.

Two main types of methods have been developed for this separation:

- Methods using the difference in the statistical signatures of these various causes of image change;
- Methods resting on explicit modelling of motion.

The second type of methods has been used by researchers who wanted to perform motion analysis for other reasons (camera work and object motion analysis), who worked from motion vector-based video coding (MPEG for instance) or who preferred these methods because of their background [54, 69]. The first type of method has been favored by researchers for which low computation time was essential. The initial methods used color histogram distance computation between successive images [63], eventually made more robust to noise and object motion by dividing the image in blocks [44] and computing distances in each block. Robustness of the detection of shot change in presence of important object motion calls for either a motion detector [55, 70] or for some type of temporal filtering of the statistical signature of image change [5, 21]. Zhang et al., proposed a method for progressive transition detection using a combination of motion and statistical analysis [70]. Purely statistical methods were refined to detect progressive effects by using properties of the distribution of pixel-to-pixel change in successive low-resolution low-passed images (Such as the DC images extracted from JPEG-coded documents). A multi-pass approach has also been proposed to improve both detection accuracy and speed [70].

Recent work has also focussed on performing shot analysis in the compressed domain. Statistical methods are easy to apply to JPEG-coded videos [14]. Some researchers [52] have written specialized DC decoders to attain better performance in extracting DC images from JPEG-coded video which does not use progressive mode. Shot analysis of MPEG-coded video can proceed along two lines:

- Direct analysis using a combination of statistical analysis between **I**-frames and **P**-frames, and motion analysis in **B**-frames [42, 54, 71].
- Efficient extraction of DC images by approximated decoding of the MPEG-flow [66].

Experiments have shown that using only I frames in detecting shot boundaries usually results in higher rate of false positives. An optimal solution will be to use both I and B frames with a combination of statistical analysis of DC images from I frames and motion vectors associated with B frames, as proposed by Zhang et al. [73]. Processing time could be further reduced while retaining high detection accuracy by using the difference between consecutive I frames as the first filter for potential shot boundaries and applying motion analysis to confirm and refine the detection [75].

It may be argued that shot analysis should be done before MPEG-encoding, since it makes possible a much better encoding. The fact that current hardware encoders do not apply it explains why researchers have nonetheless to work on shot change detection from MPEG video. It is hoped that the MPEG-4 standard will provide features that indicate shot boundaries to facilitate video indexing.

In summary, shot change detection can be reliably[2] achieved by software only methods at frame rate using today's workstations, though detecting progressive shot changes is still less reliable than detecting abrupt cut. Comparison studies of various shot change detection algorithms and schemes have been performed by Dailianas et al. [22] and Boreczky and Rowe [16]. The latter study has shown that for methods which work at the level of measures of a parameter evaluated on successive images or on differences of successive images—without any temporal filtering—histogram based algorithms outperform other algorithms.

### *3.2. Camera work and object motion analysis*

Camera work analysis in video is very useful for indexing and retrieval purposes, because it makes possible to segment long sequence shots into shorter homogeneous units defined by homogeneous camera work and can help in choosing good representative images or keyframes for a video shot. Also, some temporal filtering mechanism is necessary to eliminate camera motion noise when it is present in detecting shot changes [70]. The scientific problem of camera work analysis resides in the discrimination between camera work-induced apparent motion and object motion-induced apparent motion, followed by analysis of the camera work-induced motion in order to identify camera work. These are classical problems in computer vision, but they are made specific by the open environment (no calibrated data or knowledge about the scene contents) and by the need for very efficient computation.

Camera work analysis was first addressed through motion vector field analysis [12, 62], by matching motion vector fields to prototype models for various camera work. Very good results can be obtained by this type of analysis provided that some background/figure discrimination is used (for instance by estimating motion vectors through hierarchical block matching). Unfortunately these methods are computationally expensive, and the results obtained by direct global estimation from MPEG-type motion vectors are not very good. A simple, yet effective approach to camera work analysis has been proposed to distinguish the gradual transition sequences and classify camera pan and zoom operations [70]. The search for methods which are more computationally efficient has also lead to methods based on discrete tomography. Tonomura and Akutsu proposed to use X-ray images obtained by computing the average of each line and each column in successive images, first for representation purposes [61] and then for camera work identification [13]. A simplified approach based on the same ideas has been used by Joly and Kim [37]. The distribution of the angles of edges in the X-ray images can be matched to camera work models, and camera noise filtering, camera motion classification and temporal segmentation can be obtained directly. X-ray images can be efficiently extracted from JPEG-compressed domains by accessing only DC, $AC_{0,1}$ and $AC_{1,0}$ coefficients [51].

Some difficult problems remain to be addressed in camera work analysis. All methods fail when very large object motion cannot be discriminated from background motion, even in cases in which the semantics processing of a human viewer succeeds in doing so. Discrimination between pan and lateral travelling and between zoom and booming can be achieved only through parallax analysis.

### *3.3. Framing and focus*

The framing of a video shot (from wide shot to close shot) and its focus (narrow focus on object, total focus on the whole scene, etc.) are important parameters of video indexing as has been pointed out by Hampapur et al. [30]. Few researchers have tried to automatically recognize framing. Part of the difficulty comes from the fact that some framing types, such as a knee shot or a head-and-shoulder shot are defined in reference to the human characters present in the scene. Thus, framing analysis calls for some type of semantic analysis of images, or for finding statistical features which are strongly correlated with a given framing type. It seems that framing analysis is a reachable objective. Focus analysis can be useful not only for indexing but also by for the extraction of specially important objects in images with small depth of field. Existing defocus estimators such as those used in recovery of depth from focus [17, 22] should be applicable through some adaptation to the uncalibrated single image environment of video.

### *3.4. Video soundtrack analysis*

Though there is general agreement on the fact that sound is an essential component of video, and that image/sound relationships are critical to the perception and understanding of video contents, video soundtrack analysis is still in its infancy. So far, it has been addressed from 3 different points of view:

- Speech, music and Foley sound[3] detection, segmentation, and representation;
- Locutor identification and retrieval in speech soundtracks;
- Word spotting and labelling for speech soundtracks when a textual transcription is available (close caption or speech recognition).

Video soundtracks are often very complex, resulting from the mixing of many sound sources. From the perceptive point of view, the discrimination between speech, music and natural noises (often synthesized as artifacts in video) defines the essential structure. It turns out that detection of speech, music and their combinations in presence of various types of noise is not such an easy problem, even discarding limited cases such as grumbling, purely percussive music or recitative. Hawley [32] has designed an harmonicity detector which can be used for music detection, and after spectral substraction for speech detection when the music component has been deleted. A method for detection of isolated speech and music only, similar in its principle to Hawley's has been proposed by Wyse and Smoliar [65]. Some researchers investigate methods based on the micro-segmentation of sound signals [39] and evaluation of the degree of stationary in each micro-segment. The idea is to be able to build direct detectors of speech and music which function independently of the presence of the other component and are robust to noise.

Locutor labelling of speech segments seems to be possible through the adaptation of classical locutor identification techniques in order to train them on uncalibrated examples. It should be noted that recognition rates which would be unacceptable for identification purposes can still be very useful if the aim is to find "the next time this locutor is again present in the soundtrack".

Word spotting and speech soundtrack labelling are associated techniques (soundtrack labelling from a speech transcription reduces to a repeated word spotting problem). Speech recognition from video soundtrack is still difficult because of the presence of other sound components. The development of television programs with (unsynchronized) close captions makes soundtrack labelling particularly interesting. The Informedia project at Carnegie Mellon University is using both speech recognition techniques to convert speech into text and close caption text systematically for analyzing and abstracting news and documentary video programs [64]. Their work has shown that combining of speech, text and image analysis can provide much more information, thus, achieve higher performance in video content analysis and abstraction than any one media alone.

### 3.5. *Video scene analysis*

There can be from 500 to 1000 shots per hour in a typical moving image program. Thus, the production of a synoptical view of the video contents usable for browsing or for quick relevance assessment calls for the recognition of meaningful time segments of longer duration than a shot, or for abstracting a shot-by-shot segmentation by selecting specially relevant ones. In media production, the level immediately higher than the shot is the sequence or scene, a series of consecutive shots constituting a unit from the narrative point of view, either because they are shoot in the same location, or because they share some thematic visual contents. There are many different forms of sequences, from a field-counterfield sequence in motion picture (with many repetitions of 2 shot types interlaced with a few other shot types) to a sequence of 2 shots of outdoors reporting inserted in a TV news programs. The process of detecting video scene is analogous to paragraphing in text document analysis and requires higher level content analysis.

Two different kind of approaches have been proposed for the automatic recognition of sequences. Zhang et al. have used models of specific types of programs such as TV news [74]. They recognize (by simple image processing) specific shot types such as shots with an anchor person and an insert. They then use the model to analyze the succession of shot types and produce a segmentation in sequences. Such model or knowledge based approaches can also applied to, for instance, sport video parsing [24]. However, when we extend the application domain, we are facing the same difficulties as in computer vision.

Aigrain et al. have used rules formalizing medium perception in order to detect local (in time) clues of macroscopical change [11]. These rules refer to transition effects, shot repetition, shot setting similarity, apparition of music in the soundtrack, editing rhythm and camera work. After detection of the local clues, an analysis of their temporal organization is done in order to produce the segmentation in sequences and to choose 1 or 2 representative shots for each sequence.

In summary, video scene analysis requires higher level content analysis and one cannot expect that it can be fully automatic based on visual content analysis using current image processing and computer vision techniques. Fusion of information extraction from video, audio and close caption or transcript text analysis may be the only solution and a successful example is the Informedia Project [64].

### *3.6. Video abstraction and representation*

Considering the large amount of data necessary to code digital video, there is a high cost to video networking, both economically and in time. It is, thus, critical to offer means for quick relevance assessment of video documents. Also, while we tend to think of indexing supporting retrieval, browsing is equally significant for video source material. The task of browsing is actually very intimately related to retrieval, in formulating queries and examining retrieval results. A truly content-based approach to video browsing calls for an abstracted representation of video, even if a good index may be available (which is not the case now). How can we spend only 6 minutes to view an hour of video and still have a fairly correct perception of what its contents is like? Or how can we map an entire segment to some small number of representative images? This is the video abstracting problem. Obviously, we will not ask for the perception of the abstract to provide exhaustive information, but we would like salient features, typical style and all major subjects to be included.

***3.6.1. Video icon construction.*** The construction of a statical icon representing a video shot is one of the basic brick of video representation in a abstracted manner and is very useful in video browsing. It has attracted much work, with two major approaches:

- Construction of a visual icon based on a frame extracted from the shot, eventually supplemented with pseudo-depth for the representation of the duration of the shot, and arrows and signs for the representation of object and camera motion;
- Synthesis of an image representing the global visual contents of the shot.

The first approach has been favored when the emphasis is on building a global structured view of a video document, fitted for quick visual browsing, and when it is not deemed possible for legal or cultural reasons to modify images from the document. This approach has been used for instance in the IMPACT system [63]. Some researchers have used icon spacing or image size instead of pseudo-depth for representation of the duration of the shot[4], but this does not seem compatible with efficient screen space use. One can find examples of use of arrows and signs for representation of object and camera motion in [63].

Two interesting problems when one is using extracted frames for the representation of a video shot are image schematizing and smart shrinking. When media professionals or analysts draw (with paper and pencil) a representation of the visual contents of a shot, they outline a simplified view of the salient image features. This is a visually efficient representation and one might wonder if the same type of outlining could not be automatically produced. Unfortunately it is not an easy problem: intelligent outlining goes far beyond edge extraction. The second problem is more critical: there are limits on the resolution at which the visual contents of a video image are readable: most representations in visual interfaces use resolutions in the range $80 \times 60$ to $160 \times 120$, the upper figures being the most frequent. Occasionally, when one wants to display many images, resolutions down to $40 \times 30$ can be used, but many images become unreadable even from the global structure point of view. This creates limitations for the scope of video representations: only a limited number of shots can be simultaneously displayed, and we do not have the same type of zooming out capabilities that one finds for instance for sound visualization. It seems that it would be possible to use smarter "shrinking" strategies that the undersampling (with eventual filtering) presently used when decreasing resolution.

Teòdosio and Bender [60], and Tonomura et al. [61] have proposed methods for the automatic construction of an image representing all the visible contents of a shot. Using camera work analysis and the geometrical transformations associated to each camera motion, the successive images are mapped into a common frame, and the synthetic image is progressively built. This image is not generally rectangular. Recently, Irani et al. working in the frame of image compression, have perfected this type of method on two points [35]:

- they use a more complete projective model, including parallax;
- they have shown that it is possible to compute what they call dynamic mosaic images with privilege being given to the moving parts of the image (action) instead of background oriented images.

The resulting images have been termed *salient stills* [60], *videospaceicons* [58] and *mosaic images* [35].

Some researchers have tried to combine key frame oriented shot representation with motion traces of the type produced by salient stills, but it still unclear whether a visually convincing result can be obtained by this combination.

***3.6.2. Key-frame extraction.*** Key-frames are still images which best represent the content of the video sequence in an abstracted manner, and are extracted from original video data. Thus, key-frame based video representation views video abstraction as a problem of mapping an entire segment (both static and motion content) to some small number of representative images.

Key frames are frequently used to supplement the text of a video log [46], but there has been little work in identifying them automatically. The challenge is that the extraction of key-frames needs to be automatic and content based so that they maintain the important content of the video while remove all redundancy. In theory semantic primitives of video, such as interesting objects, actions and events should be used; however, such general semantic analysis is not currently feasible. An approach to key-frame extraction based on low-level video features has been proposed by Zhang et al. [73, 75]. In this approach, key-frames are extracted at shot level using color and brightness features of frames and their variation, and dominant motion components resulting from camera operations and large moving objects. The algorithm has also been extended into MPEG compressed domain, in which DCT coefficients of I frames and motion vectors from B and P frames are used. In addition users can adjust several parameters to control the density of key frames in each shot. A user study [73] has shown that the algorithm performed satisfactory in terms of both high accuracy and low redundancy. It is also shown that the algorithm outperforms human operator in term of consistency.

Apart from browsing, key-frames can also be used in representing video in retrieval: video index may be constructed based on visual features of key-frames, and queries may be directed at key-frames using query by image content techniques [23, 75].

***3.6.3. Video skimming.*** Video skimming is the scheme to answer the request of abstracting an hour of video, for instance, into 5 minutes highlights with a fair perception of the video contents. This is a relatively new research area and requires high level content analysis.

Joly and Kim [37] has used editing analysis to select series of shots which will be included in the abstract using rules. But, precise evaluation of the quality of the resulting abstracts has not been conducted yet. The more successful approach is to utilize information from text analysis of video soundtrack. Researchers [e.g., 58] working on documents with textual transcriptions have suggested to produce video abstracts by first abstracting the text by classical text skimming techniques and then looking for the corresponding parts in the video.

A more sophisticated approach has been proposed by the Informedia project team in which text and visual content information are fused to identify video sequences that highlight the important contents of video [31]. More specifically, low-level and mid-level visual features, including shot boundary, human face, camera and object motion and subtitles of video shots are integrated with keywords, spotted from text obtained from close caption and speech recognition, following the procedures as below:

- Keyword selection using the well-known TF-IDF[5] technique to skim audio;
- Sequence characterization by low-level and mid-level visual features;
- Selecting number of keywords according to required skimming factor;
- Prioritizing image sequences located closely to each selected keyword:
  - — Frames with faces or text;
  - — Static frames following camera motion;
  - — Frames with camera motion and human faces or text;
  - — Frame at the beginning of the scene;
- Compose a skimmed highlight sequence with selected frames.

Experiments of this skimming approach has shown impressive results on limited types of documentary video which have very explicit speech or text (close caption) contents, such as education video, news or parliament debates. However, satisfying results may not be achievable using such a text (keyword) driven approach to other videos with a soundtrack containing more than just speech, or stock footage without soundtrack.

### 3.7. *Shot similarity and content-based retrieval of clips*

Defining video shot or sequence similarity is a key issue in building content-based indices, retrieving sequences of similar visual content and clustering similar shots to construct synoptical views or visual summary. Most researchers have computed shot similarity from similarity of the images chosen to represent each shot, which obviously leaves apart all the dynamical dimension of the shots if only a single representative image is used. This can be improved by using keyframes extracted based on both static and temporal features of video [73, 75]. Based on keyframes, Yeung and Liu have recently formalized a slightly extended definition of shot similarity for shot clustering [68].

Though a set of keyframes will represent temporal content of shots to some extent, more precise measure of shot similarity should incorporate motion features, apart from features of static images. In response to such requirement, a set of statistic measures of motion features of shots has been proposed and applied in news anchor detection and shot clustering for browsing and annotation [74, 76]. However, defining more quantitative measures of shots similarity that capture the motion nature of video still remains a challenging research topic.

Techniques for the content-based retrieval of video will need much progress before they can be applied to the full search of a complete video archive. With existing techniques for feature extraction, similarity computation and explicit or implicit user query formulation, content-based retrieval of video is restricted to two already very important situations:

- finding a shot in a document;
- retrieval of single-shot clips in an archive of such clips.

The techniques described in Sections 2 and 3.7 are all applicable in order to find, for instance, the next shot which is similar from some point of view to some "present" shot. Though these techniques have been applied in some prototypes [44, 48, 75], no precise comparison between this type of navigation by visual content retrieval and direct user browsing of shot representations has been made. In-document navigation by locutor or word retrieval in soundtrack would clearly be very useful: we have already mentioned that the Informedia project plans to make it possible. For the second type of application, in the case of video stock footage, Gordon and Domeshek [25] have proposed indexing schemes which could be combined with automatic feature extraction and similarity measures in order to build a retrieval system.

### 3.8. *Visual presentation and annotation techniques for video*

Visual presentation, interactive perception and annotation of video contents raise many difficult issues. A complete treatment of the related techniques is not possible in the limits of this review. One can refer to [3] for a discussion of the adaptations in the information infrastructure which are necessary to make possible some key functionalities of interactive perception of audiovisual contents. Let us mention some interesting approaches to visual information display and user annotation techniques.

Video contents are multi-dimensional, with image, sound, and many semantic dimensions. Video representation is screen space consuming, and calls for representations at various time scales. The temporal dimension of video is particularly difficult to accommodate:

- because of the plurality of time domains (sequential time in the document, complex narrative time space),
- because the image component is better represented in a non-linear manner, i.e., using the shots or sequences as equally spaced units, whose duration is figured by pseudo-3D-depth, and the sound components are more easy to represent with a linear time-scale.

Solutions for combining non-linear time scales for image with pseudo-linear time scales for sound have been proposed by Aigrain and Joly in [6, 10]. Butler and Parkes have proposed what they call *time-space filmic diagrams* for the on-screen representation of narrative time [18].

User annotation is of course a key aspect of interactive access to video as was pointed out since the Experimental Video Annotator of Mackay and Davenport [41]. Due to the improperness of input physical devices, on-screen annotation is still very far from seriously competing with the naturalness and expressiveness of pencil annotation of a printed representation. An interesting approach to finding more adequate on-screen annotation mechanisms is icon palette annotation in which the user chooses pre-defined icons in icon palettes. Haase has proposed a model for icon palette annotation in [29].

### 3.9. *Video indexing and visual cataloging*

Traditional video indexing must be rethought in the new situation opened by the availability of content analysis techniques. In video archives and databases, 3 levels of descriptive coverage are traditionally considered:

- Minimal cataloguing with indications concerning the origin and carrier of the document, its title, duration, and more generally all information which is directly accessible on labels or package of the carrier, without any research or viewing of the document;
- More complete cataloguing with indications of various authors or contributors, eventually calling for some research or viewing of the credits in the document itself;
- Real contents indexing, for instance shot-by-shot indexing and description.

Human contents indexing is very time consuming and thus costly. It has been estimated [28] that the ratio of indexing time to document time is of the order of 10 : 1. It is, thus, used only for limited samples of particularly valuable documents, such as news archives of the broadcasting industry. Video editing analysis and representation techniques make possible a completely different organization of the video indexing process. It is now possible to build automatic storyboarding software which will produce shot-by-shot storyboard in real-time during transfer or digitizing of a document (see [10, 11] for presentations of such a software). It is thus possible for human indexers to concentrate on the truly semantic information which will not be readable on the automatically produced storyboards, and hard to retrieve for content-based retrieval systems. These storyboards can be either printed or on-line accessed. In both cases, access to a full shot-by-shot storyboard maybe too long, and synoptic representations constructed from large-scale analysis (see Section 3.5) or browsers (see below) can be used to provide users with a quicker glimpse at the document visual contents.

### *3.10. Computer-assisted video annotation and transcription*

Users who access video documents frequently need to produce speech transcriptions of the dialogues or shot-by-shot annotation, for their own use or for communication purposes. When no close caption is available, full automatic speech transcription in a multi-locutor noisy environment of continuous speech such as video is out of reach of speech recognition research. But video analysis can help in building softwares which make dialogue transcription and shot-by-shot annotation much easier. The simple fact of being able to playback a shot in a loop while typing, with easy navigation to the next of previous shots, can save time by a factor of 2 or 3 compared to transcription using a tape-recorder like software with no shot segmentation information. Pages of transcript or notes illustrated by images extracted from shots can be automatically printed or accessed on-screen [10]. When close caption is available, such pages can be automatically produced, by combining shot analysis with speech labelling. Shahraray and Gibbon [56] have developed a software which produces HTML-coded video transcripts for close-captioned news.

### *3.11. Summary*

The majority of the techniques reviewed in this section address problems in recovering low level structure of video sequences, though these techniques are basic and very useful in facilitating intelligent video browsing and search. Successful efforts in extracting semantic content are still very limited and there is a long way to go before we can achieve our goal of content-based video retrieval. On the other hand, what levels of understanding of content are most important to recover from video? Should recovering high-level intentional descriptions (what the characters are thinking or trying to do) as is needed for discourse and semantic analysis be our goal? It was observed during NSF/ARPA Workshop on Visual Information Management Systems that there seemed to be good agreement that a focus on human action is the most important topic to address over the next decade, since over 95% of all video the primary camera subject is a human or group of humans (who may be discussing some more abstract subject) [36].

On the other hand, it should be pointed out that, one of the most important points is that video content analysis, retrieval and management should *not* be thought of a fully automatic process. We should focus in developing video analysis tools to facilitate human analysts, editors and end users to manage video more intelligently and efficiently. While solving the general problem of video analysis and retrieval is difficult, we believe applications to particular needs of specific users and specific domains may be very successful.

## 4. User interfaces and browsing tools

### 4.1. *User interface for still image retrieval*

The variety of similarity types creates user interface problems for content-based retrieval of still images. It may become almost as difficult to control the retrieval process by choosing and combining similarity types as it is to formulate a textual query. Combining navigation techniques with retrieval by similarity have been suggested as a potential solution for this problem [2]. It is much easier to choose between examples of images which are similar from some point of view than to explicitly state the nature of this similarity. Images which are *dissimilar* from some point of view can also be presented: Romer [36] has pointed out that image search is also a matter of looking for an image which is "not like this one from this point of view". When similarity is computed from image descriptions and not from the image content itself, retrieval by navigation along similarity/dissimilarity links has proved to be faced with serious limits at least when the user is looking for a particular image in a large set of images [7, 8]. But looking back at similarity navigation now that feature extraction and similarity measures are more mature may be worthwhile.

Therefore, advanced user interfaces that allow relevance feedback by example, learning, and very fast browsers are essential to the success of content-based image retrieval and user and task learning or adaptation is, therefore, a key issue in image retrieval. A practical system should have the flexibility to adaptably select feature sets, similarity measures, and search methods to suit particular images. A very promising example of such methodology is the "society of models" approach proposed by Picard and Minka [50].

### 4.2. *Video browsing tools*

The volume of video data requires techniques to present information landscape or structure to give idea of what is out there. Interactive browsing of full video contents is probably the essential feature of new forms of interactive access to video. Three basic models have been proposed for video presentation and browsing:

- time-line and strata browsers;
- hierarchical browsers;
- graph browsers.

Time-line based browsers have been favored by researchers interested in video production and editing systems, for which time-line interfaces are classical. Some browsers rest on a single shot-based image component line [7, 63], but the multidimensional dimension character of video, calling for multi-line representation of the contents has been stressed by researchers working in the frame of the Muse toolkit [34, 41]. This has been systematized in the *strata* models proposed by Aguierre-Smith and Davenport [1]. Recent work on time-line browsers has focussed on combining various automatically produced lines representing a particular angle of view on the document (shots, transition effects, speech, music, Foley sounds), with user lines used for annotation. Examples of this type of browsers can be found in [11, 63]. A limitation of time-line browsers is that, since it is difficult to zoom out while keeping a good image visibility, the time-scope of what is actually displayed at a given moment on screen is relatively limited. This has lead researchers to introduce multi-scale or hierarchical aspects in the time-line browsers.

A first attempt at building hierarchical browsers—called the Video Magnifier [43] simply used successive horizontal lines each of which offered greater time detail and narrower time scope by selecting images from the document. There was no underlying structure. Recent hierarchical browsers [72] are based on levels corresponding to the actual structure of the video contents: for instance shots, sequences, scenes, etc. Shots are automatically recognized, while higher level objects are manually defined by a human indexer. The video contents are accessed as a tree each node corresponding to a segment at a given level and being represented by an image (with timing data and eventual name). Such hierarchical browsers has been further enhanced to provide similarity based browsing. That is, visual similarity of shots based on keyframes, instead of temporal relations only, are used to cluster shots automatically into scenes to provide a more content based overview at scene levels [76].

An alternative approach to hierarchical browsers has been proposed by Yeung et al. [67]. Using the clustering of visually similar shots, they construct a directed graph whose nodes are clusters of shots. Cluster A is linked to cluster B if one of the shots in A is immediately followed by a shot in B. The resulting graph is displayed for browsing, each node being represented by a key-frame extracted from one of the shots in the node. The graph can be edited for simplification by a human indexer. The drawbacks of this approach lie in the difficulty of the graph layout problem, resulting in poor screen space use, and in the fact that the linear structure of the document is no longer perceptible.

### *4.3. Playback control and computer-assisted perception*

There has been surprisingly little work on making possible new modes of playback control in interaction with video. Most systems use content analysis and representation mostly for the retrieval or visual browsing of segments, each of which is then played using simple "tape recorder-like" control panels. Researchers working on viewing systems for scholars and media specialists have proposed models and realized systems [11] in which:

- playback is synchronized with the display of cursors on the contents representation,
- temporal programming of playback of segments is possible using visual programming from examples and direct manipulation.

Temporal programming of playback is essential for the analytic and comparative perception of video. It can be combined with spatial layout, by playing back for instance two extracts of different or the same document side by side.

## 5. Conclusions

In this paper, we have reviewed to a great extent many research efforts and techniques addressing visual content representation and content based retrieval of visual data. It is clear from this survey that the number of research issues and their scope are rather large and expanding rapidly with advances in computing and communication. As a result, visual data is becoming the center of multimedia computing, and more and more researchers from different fields are attracted and start to explore these issues. On the other hand, how to extract and manage semantics information of visual data remains a major bottleneck, which call for not only more research efforts, but most critically right research approaches.

An application-oriented approach is critical to the success of visual data representation and retrieval researches and will prevent it from being too theoretical. By working on strongly focused applications, the research issues reviewed in this paper can be addressed in the context of well defined applications and will facilitate the applications, while achieving general solutions remains long term research topics.

When we strive for visual content analysis and representation, it should be pointed out again that integration of different information sources, such as speech, sound and text is as important as visual data itself in understanding and indexing visual data. Keywords and conceptual retrieval techniques are and will always be an important part of visual information systems. What we should focus on should include techniques to help annotation of image and video, and other meta-data.

## Notes

1. This work was performed while this author was with Institute of Systems Science, Singapore.
2. With an error rate comparable to human indexing.
3. Foley sounds, named after Jack Foley [1891–1967], sound engineer for Universal Studios, are artifically produced sounds imitating natural noises. There are databases of Foley sounds and similar natural or instrumental sounds and indexing and retrieval in these databases has lead to interesting research [15].
4. One can find examples of use of image spacing or size for representation of duration in drawn storyboards; see [47].
5. TF-IDF technique: Term Frequency Inverse Document Frequency.

## References


1. T.G. Aguierre-Smith and G. Davenport, "The stratification system: A design environment for random access video," Proc. 3rd Int. Workshop on Network and Operating System Support for Digital Audio and Video, La Jolla, CA, USA, Nov. 1992, pp. 250–261.
2. P. Aigrain, "Organizing image banks for visual access: Model and techniques," OPTICA'87 Conf. Proc., Amsterdam, Learned Information, April 1987, pp. 257–270.
3. P. Aigrain, "Image and sound digital libraries need more than storage and networked access," Proc. International Symposium on Digital Libraries, ULIS, Tsukuba, Japan, Aug. 1995, pp. 112–118.
4. P. Aigrain, "Software research for video libraries and archives," IFLA Journal, special issue on the UNESCO Memory of the World Project, Vol. 21, No. 3, pp. 198–202, 1995.
5. P. Aigrain and P. Joly, "The automatic real-time analysis of film editing and transition effects and its applications," Computers & Graphics, Vol. 18, No. 1, pp. 93–103, Jan.–Feb. 1994.
6. P. Aigrain and P. Joly, "Discrete visual manipulation user interfaces for video," Proc. RIAO'94 Conference, New-York, Oct. 1994, Vol. 2, pp. 12–17.
7. P. Aigrain and V. Longueville, "A connection graph for user navigation in a large image bank," Proc. RIAO'91, Barcelona, Spain, April 1991, Vol. 1, pp. 67–84.
8. P. Aigrain and V. Longueville, "Evaluation of navigational links between images," Information Processing and Management, Vol. 28, No. 4, pp. 517–528, 1992.

9. P. Aigrain, P. Joly, and V. Longueville, "Medium-knowledge-based macro-segmentation of video into sequences," Working Notes of IJCAI Workshop on Intelligent Multimedia Information Retrieval, Montreal, Aug. 1995, pp. 5–14.
10. P. Aigrain, P. Joly, H.-K. Kim, and P. Lepain, Software Tools for Moving Image Archives: Access, Indexing and User Interfaces, G. Boston (Ed.), Proc. Joint Technical Sympoisum on Technology and Our Audiovisual Heritage, FIAF/FIAT/IASA/IFLA/ICA, London, Jan. 1995.
11. P. Aigrain, P. Joly, P. Lepain, and V. Longueville, "Representation-based user interfaces for the audiovisual library of year 2000," Proc. IS&T/SPIE'95 Multimedia Computing and Networking, San Jose, Feb. 1995, pp. 35–45.
12. A. Akutsu, Y. Tonomura, H. Hashimoto, and Y. Ohba, "Video indexing using motion vectors," Proc. Visual Communication and Image Processing, SPIE, Amsterdam, 1992, Vol. 1818, pp. 1522–1530.
13. A. Akutsu and Y. Tonomura, "Video tomography: An efficient method for camerawork extraction and motion analysis," Proc. A.C.M. Multimedia Conference, San Francisco, Oct. 1994.
14. F. Arman, A. Hsu, and M.Y. Chiu, "Feature management for large video databases," Proc. Storage and Retrieval for Image and Video Databases I, SPIE, Feb. 1993, Vol. 1908, pp. 2–12.
15. T. Blum, D. Keislar, J. Wheaton, and E. Wold, "Audio databases with content-based retrieval," Working Notes of IJCAI Workshop on Intelligent Multimedia Information Retrieval, Montreal, Aug. 1995, pp. 71–92.
16. J.S. Boreczky and L.A. Rowe, "Comparison of video shot boundary detection techniques," Proc. SPIE Conf. Storage and Retrieval for Video Databases IV, San Jose, CA, USA, Feb. 1995.
17. V.M. Bove, Jr., "Entropy-based depth from focus," Journal of the Optical Society of America A, Vol. 10, pp. 561–566, April 1993.
18. S. Butler and A.P. Parkes, "Filmic spacetime diagrams for video structure representation," to appear in Image Communication special issue on Image and Video Semantics: Processing, Analysis and Application, 1996.
19. N.-S. Chang and K.-S. Fu, "Query by pictorial example," IEEE Transactions on Software Engineering, Vol. 6, No. 6, pp. 519–524, Nov. 1980.
20. M. Cherfaoui and C. Bertin, "Two-stage strategy for indexing and presenting video," Proc. SPIE Conf. Storage and Retrieval for Video Databases III, San Jose, CA, USA, Feb. 1994, Vol. 2185.
21. A. Dailianas, R. Allen, and P. England, "Comparison of automatic video segmentation algorithms," Proceedings of SPIE Photonics West, Philadelphia, Oct. 1995.
22. J. Ens and P. Lawrence, "An investigation of methods determining depth from focus," IEEE Transactions on Pattern Matching and Machine Intelligence, Vol. 15, pp. 97–108, Feb. 1993.
23. M. Flickner et al., "Query by image and video content," IEEE Computer, pp. 23–32, Sept. 1995.
24. Y. Gong, L.T. Sin, H.C. Chuan, H.J. Zhang, and M. Sakauchi, "Automatic parsing of TV soccer programs," Proc. Second IEEE International Conference on Multimedia Computing and Systems, Washington DC, May 15–18, 1995, pp. 167–174.
25. A.S. Gordon and E.A. Domeshek, "Conceptual indexing for video retrieval," Working Notes of IJCAI Workshop on Intelligent Multimedia Information Retrieval, Montreal, Aug. 1995, pp. 23–38.
26. V.N. Gudivada, "On spatial similarity measures for multimedia applications," Proc. SPIE Conf. Storage and Retrieval for Image and Video Databases III, San Jose, CA, USA, Feb. 1994, Vol. 2420, pp. 363–380.
27. V.N. Gudivada and V.V. Raghavan, "Design and evaluation of algorithms for image retrieval by spatial similarity," ACM Transactions on Information Systems, Vol. 13, No. 2, pp. 115–144, April 1995.
28. V. Guigueno, "L'identité de l'image: Expression et systémes documentaires," rapport d'option, Ecole Polytechnique, Palaiseau, France, Juillet, 1991.
29. K. Haase, "Framer: A persistent portable representation library," Proc. of ECAI'94, 1994.
30. A. Hampapur, R. Jain, and T.E. Weymouth, "Production model based digital video segmentation," Multimedia Tools and Applications, Vol. 1, No. 1, pp. 9–46, 1995.
31. A.G. Hauptmann and M. Smith, "Text, speech and vision for video segmentation: The Informedia project," Working Notes of IJCAI Workshop on Intelligent Multimedia Information Retrieval, Montreal, Aug. 1995, pp. 17–22.
32. M. Hawley, Structure Out of Sound, Ph.D. Dissertation, MIT Media Laboratory, Cambridge, Mass., USA, 1993.
33. K. Hirata and T. Kato, "Query by Visual Example: Content-Based Image Retrieval," Proc. E.D.B.T.'92 Conf. on Advances in Database Technology, in Pirotte, Delobel, and Gottlob (Eds.), Springer-Verlag, Lecture Notes in Computer Science, Vol. 580, pp. 56–71, 1994.

34. M.E. Hodges, R.M. Sassnett, and M.S. Ackerman, "A construction set for multimedia applications," IEEE Software, pp. 37–43, Jan. 1989.
35. M. Irani, P. Anandan, J. Bergen, R. Kumar, and S. Hsu, "Mosaic based representations of video sequences and their applications," Image Communication special issue on Image and Video Semantics: Processing, Analysis and Application, 1996.
36. R. Jain, A. Pentland, and D. Petkovic (Eds.), Workshop Report: NSF-ARPA Workshop on Visual Information Management Systems, Cambridge, Mass., USA, June 1995.
37. P. Joly and H.-K. Kim, "Efficient automatic analysis of camera work and micro-segmentation of video using spatio-temporal images," Image Communication special issue on Image and Video Semantics: Processing, Analysis and Application, 1996.
38. T. Kato, "Database architecture for content-based image retrieval," Proc. of SPIE Conf. on Image Storage and Retrieval Systems, San Jose, Feb. 1992, Vol. 1662, pp. 112–123.
39. P. Lepain and R. André-Obrecht, "Micro-segmentation d'enregistrements musicaux," Actes des Journées d'Informatique Musicale, Vol. 95-13, pp. 81–90, 1995.
40. W.E. Mackay and G. Davenport, "Virtual video editing in interactive multimedia applications," Communications of the A.C.M., Vol. 32, No. 9, July 1989.
41. J. Meng, Y. Juan, and S.-F. Chang, "Scene change detection in an MPEG compressed video sequence," IS&T/SPIE'95 Digital Video Compression: Algorithm and Technologies, San Jose, Feb. 1995, Vol. 2419, pp. 14–25.
42. M. Mills, J. Cohen, and Y.Y. Wong, "A magnifier tool for video data," Proc. INTERCHI'92, ACM, May 1992, pp. 93–98.
43. A. Nagasaka and Y. Tanaka, "Automatic scene-change detection method for video works," E. Knuth and I.M. Wegener (Eds.), Proc. 40th National Con. Information Processing Society of Japan, 1990.
44. A. Nagasaka and Y. Tanaka, Automatic Video Indexing and Full-Search for Video Appearances, E. Knuth and I.M. Wegener (Eds.), Visual Database Systems, Elsevier Science Publishers: Amsterdam, Vol. II, pp. 113–127, 1992.
45. B.C. O'Connor, "Selecting key frames of moving image documents: A digital environment for analysis and navigation," Microcomputers for Information Management, Vol. 8, No. 2, pp. 119–133, 1991.
46. B. Peeters, J. Faton, and P. de Pierpont, Storyboard-Le Cinéma Dessiné, Editions Yellow Now, 1992.
47. A. Pentland, R.W. Picard, and S. Sclaroff, "Photobook: Content-based manipulation of image databases," Proc. Storage and Retrieval for Image and Video Databases II, San Jose, CA, USA, Feb. 1994, Vol. 2185.
48. R. Picard and Fang Liu, "A new World ordering for image similarity," Proc. Int. Conf. on Acoustic Signals and Signal Processing, Adelaide, Australia, March 1994, Vol. 5, p. 129.
49. R.W. Picard and T.O. Minka T., "Vision texture for annotation," Multimedia Systems, ACM-Springer, Vol. 3, No. 3, pp. 3–14, Feb. 1995.
50. F. Salazar, "Analyse automatique des mouvements de caméra dans un document vid'eo," IRIT, rapport de recherche, 95-33-R, Universit'e Paul Sabatier, Toulouse, France, Sept. 1995.
51. F. Salazar and F. Valéro, "Analyse automatique de documents vidéo," IRIT, rapport de recherche, 95-28-R, Université Paul Sabatier, Toulouse, France, Juin 1995.
52. S. Sclaroff and A. Pentland, "Modal matching for correspondence and recognition," IEEE Transactions on Pattern Analysis and Machine Intelligence, Vol. 17, No. 6, pp. 545–561, June 1995.
53. I.K. Sethi and N. Patel, "A statistic approach to scene change detection," Proc. SPIE Storage and Retrieval for Image and Video Databases III, San Jose, CA, USA, Feb. 1995, Vol. 2420, pp. 329–338.
54. B. Shahraray, "Scene change detection and content-based sampling of video sequences," IS&T/SPIE'95 Digital Video Compression: Algorithm and Technologies, San Jose, Feb. 1995, Vol. 2419, pp. 2–13, SPIE Proceedings.
55. B. Shahraray and D.C. Gibbon, "Automatic generation of pictorial transcripts of video programs," IS&T/SPIE'95 Digital Video Compression: Algorithm and Technologies, San Jose, Feb. 1995, Vol. 2417, pp. 512–519, SPIE Proceedings.
56. M. Stricker and M. Orengo, "Similarity of color images," Proc. Storage and Retrieval for Image and Video Databases III, San Jose, CA, USA, Feb. 1995, Vol. 2420, pp. 381–392, SPIE Conference Proceedings.
57. A. Takeshita, T. Inoue, and K. Tanaka, "Extracting text skim structures for multimedia browsing," in M. Maybury (Ed.), Working Notes of IJCAI Workshop on Intelligent Multimedia Information Retrieval, Montreal, Aug. 1995, pp. 46–58.

58. H. Tamura, S. Mori, and T. Yamawaki, "Texture features corresponding to visual perception," IEEE Trans. on Syst., Man, and Cybern.,Vol. 6, No. 4, pp. 460–473, 1979.
59. L. Teodosio and W. Bender, "Salient video stills: Content and context preserved," Proc. ACM Multimedia'93, Anaheim, CA, USA, Aug. 1993.
60. Y. Tonomura, A. Akutsu, K. Otsuji, and T. Sadakata, "VideoMAP and VideoSpaceIcon: Tools for anatomizing video content," Proc. InterChi'93, ACM, 1993, pp. 131–136.
61. Y.T. Tse and R.L. Baker, "Global zoom/pan estimation and compensation for video compression," Proc. ICASSP'91, May 1991, Vol. 4.
62. H. Ueda, T. Miyatake, and S. Yoshisawa, "IMPACT: An interactive natural-motion-picture dedicated multimedia authoring system," Proc. CHI'91, ACM, 1991, pp. 343–350.
63. H.D. Wactlar, D. Christel, A. Hauptmann, T. Kanade, M. Mauldin, R. Reddy, M. Smith, and S. Stevens, "Technical challenges for the informedia digital video library," Proc. International Symposium on Digital Libraries, Tsukuba, Japan, Aug. 1995, pp. 10–16.
64. L. Wyse and S.W. Smoliar, "Towards content-based audio indexing and retrieval," Proc. IJCAI Workshop on Computational Auditory Scene Analysis, D. Rosenthal and H.G. Okuno (Eds.), Montréal, Aug. 1995, pp. 149–152.
65. B.-L. Yeo and B. Liu, "On the extraction of DC sequence from MPEG compressed video," International Conference on Image Processing (ICIP'95), Washington, DC, USA, Oct. 1995, IEEE.
66. M.M. Yeung, B.-L. Yeo, W. Wolf, and B. Liu, "Video browsing using clustering and scene transitions on compressed sequences," IS&T/SPIE'95 Multimedia Computing and Networking, San Jose, Feb. 1995, Vol. 2417, pp. 399–413.
67. M.M. Yeung and B. Liu, "Efficient matching and clustering of video shots," International Conference on Image Processing (ICIP'95), Washington, DC, USA, Oct. 1995, IEEE.
68. R. Zabih, K. Mai, and J. Miller, "A robust method for detecting cuts and dissolves in video sequences," Proc. ACM Multimedia'95, San Francisco, Nov. 1995.
69. H.J. Zhang, A. Kankanhalli, and S.W. Smoliar, "Automatic partitioning of full-motion video," Multimedia Systems, ACM-Springer, Vol. 1, No. 1, pp. 10–28, 1993.
70. H.J. Zhang and S.W. Smoliar, "Developing power tools for video indexing and retrieval," Proc. SPIE'94 Storage and Retrieval for Video Databases, San Jose, CA, USA, Feb. 1994.
71. H.J. Zhang, S.W. Smoliar, and J.H. Wu, "Content-based video browsing tools," Proceedings of IS&T/SPIE'95 Multimedia Computing and Networking, San Jose, Feb. 1994, Vol. 2417.
72. H.J. Zhang, C.Y. Low, Y. Gong, and S.W. Smoliar, "Video parsing using compressed data," Proc. SPIE'94 Image and Video Processing II, San Jose, CA, USA, Feb. 1994, pp. 142–149.
73. H.J. Zhang, S.Y. Tan, S.W. Smoliar, and Y. Gong, "Automatic parsing and indexing of news video," Multimedia Systems, Vol. 2, No. 6, pp. 256–265, 1995.
74. H.J. Zhang, C.Y. Low, S.W. Smoliar, and J.H. Wu, "Video parsing, retrieval and browsing: An integrated and content-based solution," Proc. ACM Multimedia'95, San Francisco, Nov. 5–9, 1995, pp. 15–24.
75. D. Zhong, H.J. Zhang, and S.-F. Chang, "Clustering methods for video browsing and annotation," Proc. Storage and Retrieval for Image and Video Databases IV, San Jose, CA, USA, Feb. 1995.

**Philippe Aigrain** graduated in computer science from University of Toulouse, and holds a "Doctorat" in theoretical computer science from University Paris 7 (1980). In 1982 he was a research fellow at University of

California, Berkeley. Since 1983, he has been conducting research on image and sound archives and interaction with audiovisual media. He is presently head of the Media Analysis and Interaction research group in the Institut de Recherche en Informatique de Toulouse, France. His research interests are in content analysis of video and musical recordings and discrete manipulation interfaces for time-based media.

**HongJiang Zhang** obtained his Ph.D. from the Technical University of Denmark in 1991, B.Sc. in 1982 from Zhengzhou University, Zhengzhou, China, both in Electrical Engineering. From December, 1991, he has been with the Institute of Systems Science, National University of Singapore, led the work on video/image content analysis, representation indexing and retrieval. He joined the Broadband Information System Lab. of Hewlett-Packard Labs., Palo Alto, in October, 1995. His current research interests are in video/image content analysis and retrieval, interactive video, and image processing. He has published over 40 papers and book chapters in these areas and is a co-author of "Image and Video Processing in Multimedia Systems", a book published by Kluwer Academic Publishers. He serves on program committees of several international conferences on multimedia. He is also a member of the Editorial board of Kluwer's international journal "Multimedia Tools and Applications".

**Dragutin Petkovic** is the manager of the Advanced Algorithms, Architectures and Applications Department at IBM Almaden Research Center. Despite all the managerial responsibilities, he is still involved in marketing, applications, and testing much of the software his group creates. His research interests include image analysis applied to industrial, commercial, and biomedical problems, content-based search, large-image and multimedia databases, and advanced user interfaces.

Multimedia Tools and Applications, 3, 203–223 (1996)


# COMIB: Composite Icon Browser for Multimedia Databases

JAEHYUK CHA jhcha@comp.snu.ac.kr
SUKHO LEE shlee@comp.snu.ac.kr
*Department of Computer Engineering, Seoul National University, Seoul 151-742*

**Editor:** HongJiang Zhang

**Abstract.** COMIB(COMposite Icon Browser) is a graphical user interface for retrieval of multimedia databases. It gives users the effect of browsing and navigating multimedia objects simultaneously in a screen using **composite icons**, that may be thumbnails of the several nested attribute values of those objects. Users can specify these attributes with a mouse while browsing the visualized aggregation hierarchy. Both querying and browsing can be interleaved via query reformulation. We show how these features of COMIB overcome the three drawbacks of the browsing paradigm such as no overview of many objects, the repetitious short-sighted navigation, and the weak presentation of a multimedia object. We also explain the retrieval mechanism algebraically and describe the implementation of COMIB based on this mechanism.

**Keywords:** Multimedia Database, Browsing, Composite Icon

## 1. Introduction

A multimedia object is a composite object that refers to various kinds of media objects such as image, graphic, audio, and video [23]. It is not always easy to describe these media objects using a formal query language. Browsing through a large set of multimedia objects is sometimes a more efficient way for a user to find what he wants. It complements the weak querying capability on the above media objects with human cognitive capability and allows users to navigate through the database without any deep knowledge of the query language and the organization of the database [9, 14]. Thus, for efficient retrieval of multimedia databases, a combination of set-oriented querying and navigation-oriented browsing techniques is needed [5].

There are several drawbacks of browsing paradigm not complemented by querying, such as no overview of many objects [2], the repetitious short-sighted navigation [18], and the weak presentation of a multimedia object. A number of attempts to enhance the browsing method have been reported in the literatures [1, 2, 4, 6, 7, 8, 9, 11, 12, 14, 15, 16, 17, 18, 19, 20, 21, 22, 24], which will be analyzed in Section 2, but none of them succeeds in overcoming the above three drawbacks altogether.

In order to overcome all of the above drawbacks, this paper proposes COMIB (COMposite Icon Browser) that provides facilities of not only the object browsing and querying, but also the composite icon browsing and schema browsing. The features of these facilities are as follows:

- Composite Icon Browsing: Without repetitious navigation, users can see the overview of objects and their referred objects in a screen, via composite icons. This gives users the effect of browsing and navigating through multimedia objects simultaneously.
- Schema Browsing: To understand the conceptual structure of multimedia objects, the user can incrementally visualize the entire aggregation hierarchy of a class as a tree, which is similar to the iterative refinements approach [2]. On the visualized aggregation hierarchy, the user can directly specify the nested attributes, which will be used for building up the composite icons.
- Object Browsing: Within the presentation of an entire object, the referred object is displayed as a composite icon rather than an OID(object identifier), an object name, or a class name. It will enhance the visualization of the content of the object.
- Querying: During a retrieval session, querying and browsing can be interleaved in a screen. Therefore, the number of objects to browse can be controlled by the query reformulation.

We have designed an execution mechanism of COMIB algebraically and implemented a prototype based on this mechanism.

The rest of this paper is organized as follows. Section 2 describes and compares the related work. Section 3 explains an extension of the object-oriented data model for the default composite icons, and introduces the concept of a composite icon. Section 4 describes the main features of COMIB by an informal presentation of the entire retrieval session, and shows these features overcome three drawbacks of the browsing paradigm. Section 5 describes the retrieval mechanism of COMIB algebraically and Section 6 reports the current implementation. Finally, we present conclusions in Section 7.

## 2. Related Work

Currently most DBMS browsers use the table-based presentation for several objects, and the form-based presentation for an object [13]. But, when browsing multimedia objects that contain various kinds of mono-media objects along the complex structure, a number of problems occur.

One problem is the repetitious short-sighted navigation [2]. In order to see several nested attribute values of each object, users must repetitiously navigate from each object to its referred objects along the paths of those attributes. OdeView [1], KIVIEW [15], and Pasta-3 [8] try to solve this problem using the synchronized browsing method that automatically displays the referred objects of the currently displayed object according to the specified path. VILD [11], UniSQL/X [22], and $O_2$Tools [16] display an object and its referred object together on the E-R diagram, the aggregation hierarchy graph, and the nested form, respectively. Since these systems except Pasta-3 cannot display several objects simultaneously in a screen, users have to repeat the browsing work as many times as the number of objects. On the other hand, the object presentation form of Pasta-3, integrated form of tree and table, cannot deal with the multimedia objects.

Another problem is that users cannot see many objects simultaneously on a screen [18]. Because of the screen size, the form-based presentation can deal with a few number of objects at a time. The table-based presentation cannot effectively represent the mono-media objects such as image and video because these media need a 2-dimensional space. One approach to solve this problem is to use an icon browsing method [4, 6, 18]. An icon is the thumbnail of an object, for example, a miniature of the first page of an object or a smaller image instead of the full resolution image. However, it might not convey the meaningful information such as the complex structure of the object to users. There are other approaches such as Fisheye view [19], Tree-Maps [20], Perspective Wall [12], and Cone Trees [17], which provide various presentation techniques for graphs. It is difficult to apply them to database browsing because all of them cannot reduce the users' burden such as repetition of short-sighted navigation.

When browsing multimedia objects, a user might want to see a conceptual schema for a better understanding of the information space. There have been some attempts to build browsers that present the objects and their aggregation hierarchy together, in a graph [7, 8, 11, 22], or a nested form [9, 16, 25]. But, because of the limited screen size, any presentation format cannot fully show a multimedia object and its many referred objects together on a screen. Within the presentation of a multimedia object, several referred objects are displayed as the object name, the OID, or the class name instead of their data. It is difficult for the user to understand the content of the object without navigation.

In order to overcome the above drawbacks altogether, MediaBench [21] provides three modes of browsing: overview, content, structure, but for the video objects only. UniSQL/X [22] and $O_2$Tools [16] provide two modes of browsing: browsing through the graph and icons, browsing through the nested form and icons, respectively. But, as mentioned before, these two systems can solve only the short-sighted navigation for each object, not the repetitious navigation for all objects. So far, none of them succeeds in overcoming all of the above drawbacks.

## 3. Preliminaries

### *3.1. Data Model and Its Extension*

Object-oriented data model is an elegant basis for addressing all multimedia data modeling requirements such as type extensibility for new media and the support of methods for the intrinsic operations of mono-media [23]. This model is based on a number of basic concepts, namely object, identity, class, aggregation, inheritance [3].

Any real-world entity is represented as an object. Objects are categorized into classes. All objects of a given class have a common range of states and common behavior associated with them. The state of an object is defined by the values of its attributes. An attribute can have as a value both a primitive object, such as strings, integers or booleans, and a non-primitive object in turn consists of a set of attributes. Therefore, objects can be recursively defined in terms of other objects. The behavior of an object is specified by the methods that operate on the object state. And each object is uniquely identified by an OID(Object IDentifier).

A class *C* consists of a number of attributes, and the value of an attribute a of an object of class *C* is the object or the collection of objects belonging to some other class *C'*. The class *C'* in turn consists of attributes, and their domains are other classes. The fact that class *C'* is the domain of an attribute of class *C* establishes an aggregation relationship between the two classes. Aggregation relationships among classes in an object-oriented database organize classes in an aggregation hierarchy.

Classes are also organized in an inheritance hierarchy. The inheritance hierarchy is orthogonal to the aggregation hierarchy. Inheritance allows a class, called a subclass, to be defined as a specialization of other class(es), called superclass(es). A subclass inherits attributes and methods from its superclass(es), and can have its own attributes and methods.

Figure 1 illustrates sample classes of a university database schema that will be used in the remainder of the paper. An attribute of any class but the root class on an aggregation hierarchy is logically an attribute of the root class of the hierarchy, that is, the attribute is a **nested attribute** of the root class. In general, a nested attribute is denoted as a path expression, $a_1.a_2.\cdots.a_n$, that is a sequence of non-nested attribute names along the aggregation hierarchy of a class. Here, $a_i(1 \leq i < n)$ is the name of a tuple-valued attribute or a multi-valued attribute. For example, when the aggregation hierarchy of class *Student* contains classes *Department*, *Career*, *Professor*, and *Course*, the inherited attribute, 'picture' of *Professor* becomes the nested attribute of *Student*, denoted as 'advisor.picture'. And if the domain of a nested or non-nested attribute is one of primitive classes or mono-media classes, the attribute is a **presentable attribute**.

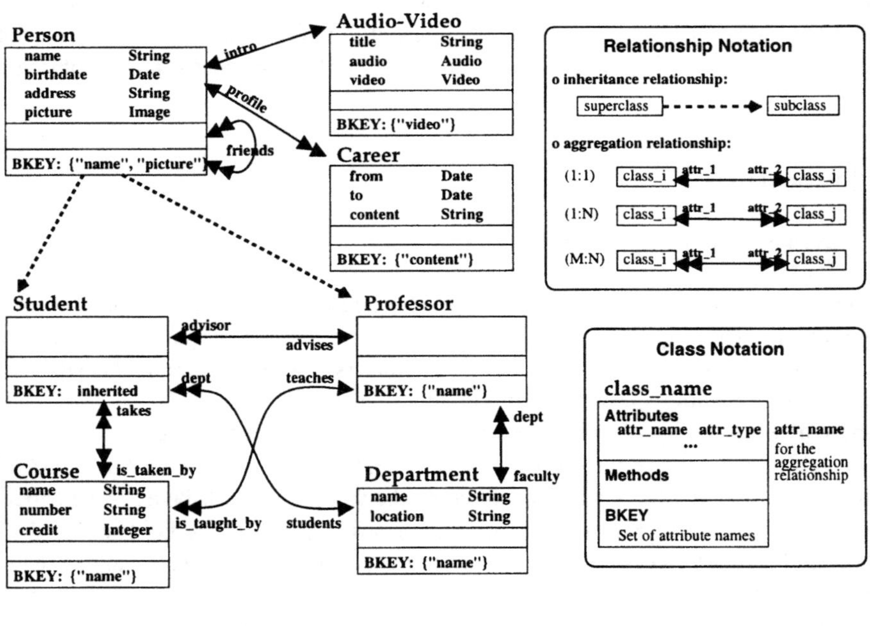


*Figure 1.* University Database Schema

In defining a new class, each attribute must be explicitly specified whether it has BKEY (Browsing KEY) characteristic or not. Any attribute, inherited or newly defined, can be a BKEY. The BKEY attributes of a class are used for displaying initial composite icons. A class without any defined BKEY attribute inherits this characteristics from its superclass(es). Thus, in case of class *Student*, inherited attributes 'name' and 'picture' have BKEY characteristic.

### 3.2. *Basic Terms*

In general, an icon typically presents a symbol of a domain type, some non-nested attribute values, or the first page of an object. However, with these icons, various kinds of aspects of multimedia objects, specially complex structure, can't be effectively represented. For this reason, we extend the icon as follows.

**DEFINITION 1 (composite icon)** *A composite icon is a miniaturized presentation of data projected from an object according to a set of presentable attributes.* □

For associating composite icons to objects of a class, the mapping information based on the class is needed. This information is defined as follows.

**DEFINITION 2 (composite icon path)** *A composite icon path is a set of presentable attributes used for making up a composite icon from an object. If a nested attribute, $a_1.a_2.\cdots.a_n$, is in a composite icon path, the type of $a_n$ should be either a primitive class or a media class. And if $a_i (1 \leq i < n)$ is the name of a multi-valued attribute, the first element is selected implicitly.* □

According to the above definitions, a nested attribute can also be an element of a composite icon path, and a composite icon can represent various kinds of aspects of a multimedia object better. For instance, Figure 2 illustrates the relationship between the retrieved objects and the composite icons of class *Student* when the composite icon path consists of the attributes 'name', 'picture', and 'advisor.picture'.

In order to specify a composite icon path of a class, it is required to know about the aggregation hierarchy of the class. For this reason, it is difficult for a novice user to specify the composite icon path. But, the COMIB supports a default composite icon path defined as follows.

**DEFINITION 3 (default composite icon path)** *For a class T, the default composite icon path comprises its BKEY attributes.* □

For instance, as shown in Figure 1, the default composite icon path of class *Student* consists of two inherited BKEY attributes, 'name' and 'picture'. These attributes are used for displaying the initial composite icons of *Student* objects.

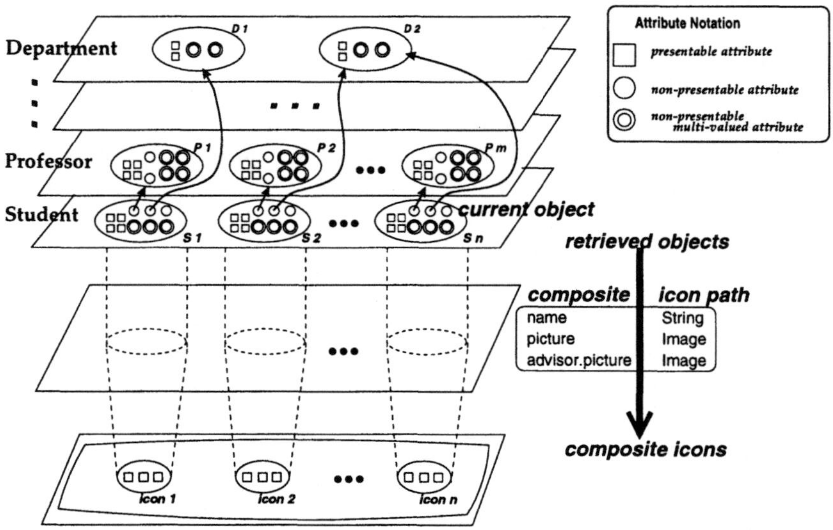


*Figure 2.* Object Flow of Composite Icon Browsing

## 4. Overview of COMIB

The entire retrieval work of COMIB(COMposite Icon Browser) consists of three execution steps. In the first step, the facility of querying is used. In the second step, these facilities of composite icon browsing and schema browsing are used. And in the last step, the facility of object browsing is used. We will show how the four facilities of COMIB can overcome the three drawbacks of browsing paradigm by an example retrieval session according to the execution steps. Figure 3 shows the screen layout of COMIB that consists of three tiled subwindows and one pop-up subwindow, each of which supports one of the above four facilities respectively. Since these subwindows are seamlessly integrated, the system enables users to efficiently interleave these facilities during a retrieval session.

The top left subwindow is a query window that allows users to specify a query statement, and displays the status information and error messages in the message area. The bottom left subwindow is an icon window that displays the composite icons of the query result and allows users to select one of those icons. Then the corresponding object is presented fully in the right subwindow called an object window. The pop-up subwindow is a composite icon path window that visualizes a current composite icon path and an aggregation hierarchy. And it allows users to directly specify a new composite icon path on the visualized aggregation hierarchy.

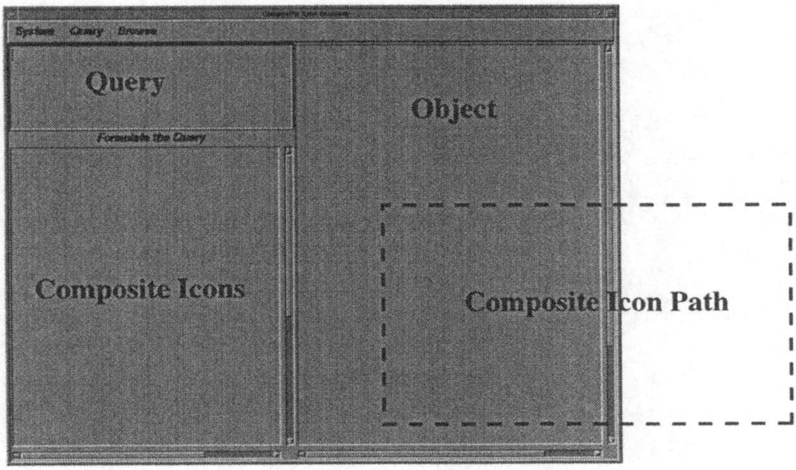


*Figure 3.* Screen layout of COMIB

### *4.1. Step 1: Querying*

Querying is good for a set-oriented search where browsing does not work well, and it can reduce the number of objects to browse. On the other hand, browsing helps users to gain insights on the contents and organization of the database, which is important for the query formulation. The COMIB is intended to interleave navigation-oriented browsing with set-oriented querying using the query reformulation.

The main activity of the first step is textual query formulation and execution. In the query window(Figure 3), the user may formulate the query, and get a set of objects. If the user is not satisfied with the result, he can reformulate the query and resubmit the modified query to the DBMS. For example, in order to search the students belonging to the department of computer engineering, the user may formulate the query as shown in the top left subwindow of Figure 4, "Select s From Student s Where s.dept.name='Computer Engineering'".

### *4.2. Step 2: Composite Icon Browsing and Schema Browsing*

Browsing multimedia objects in our system can be achieved in two different styles: composite icon browsing and object browsing. The latter is the traditional browsing method that allows users to browse and navigate the multimedia objects one by one. But, as mentioned in Section 2, this method has three drawbacks, namely no overview of many objects, the repetitious short-sighted navigation, and the weak presentation of a multimedia object. The icon browsing method, the synchronized browsing method, and the schema browsing method can only solve one of drawbacks each, not all the drawbacks altogether.

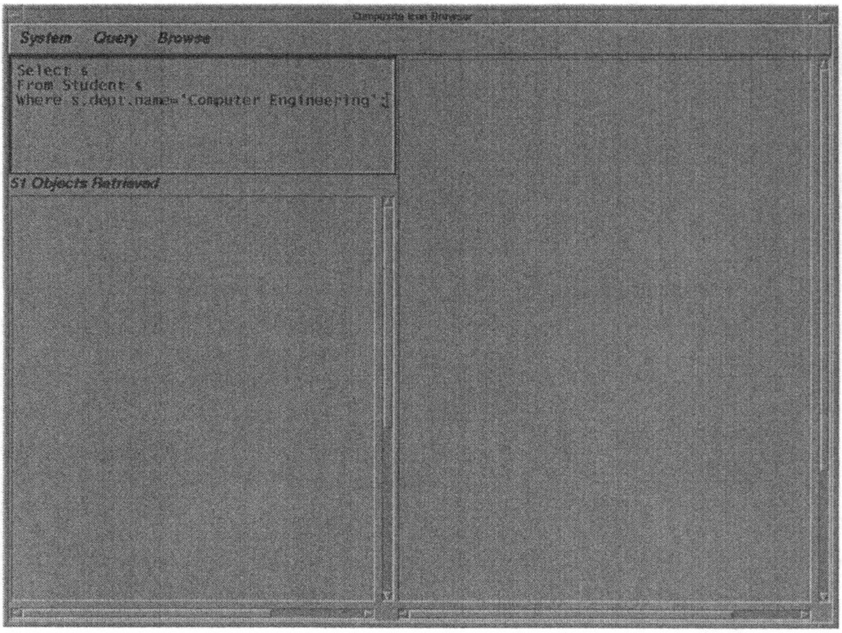


*Figure 4.* Formulation and Execution of Query

In order to solve these drawbacks altogether, we enhance the icon browsing method in three ways. First, a composite icon represents several simple or nested attribute values of an object. It will make each icon represent the corresponding composite objects more expressively. Second, with the given objects, users can scan the various kinds of composite icons using the composite icon path. It gives users the effect of navigating the corresponding objects simultaneously on the screen. Third, the schema browsing method is used for visualizing and direct modifying the composite icon path.

The above mentioned browsing methods, namely the composite icon browsing method and the schema browsing method, are used in the second step. When the user gets objects as the query result, his request of icon browsing invokes the presentation of composite icons, each of which consists of data projected from an object according to the current composite icon path. For example, the bottom left subwindow of Figure 5 shows the composite icons associated with the given objects of class *Student* according to the default composite icon path, {'name','picture'}.

Since a composite icon consists of several mono-media icons, each mono-media class should have its own miniaturizing technique. For a text class, the first five letters of an instance are displayed. For an image class, a smaller image is displayed instead of the full resolution image. For an audio class, the symbol of the speaker is displayed. When users select a composite icon containing the audio data with the right button of a mouse, the first

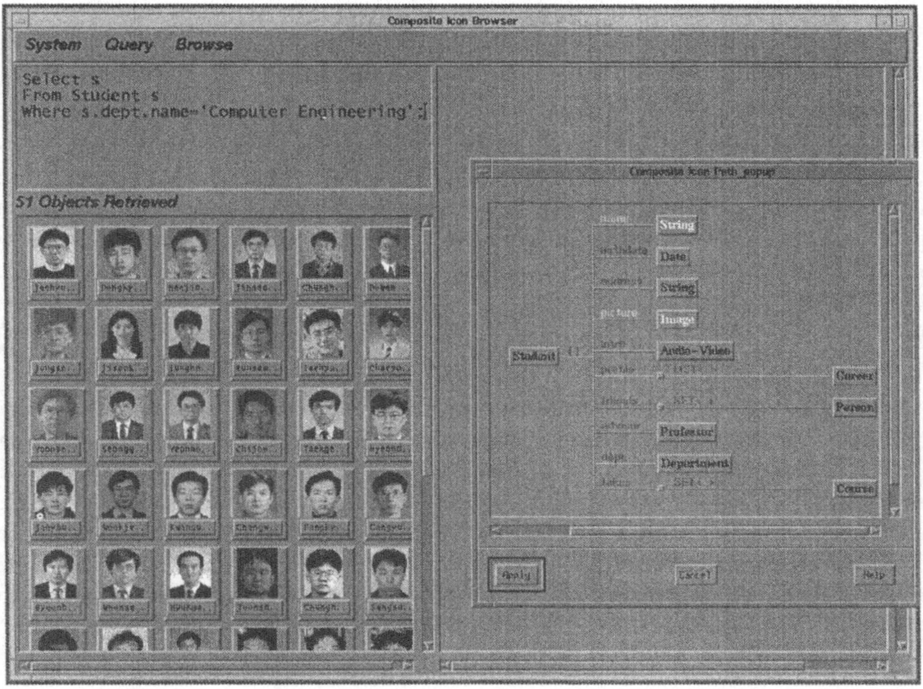


*Figure 5.* Browsing Composite Icons of Query Result

seven seconds of the data are played to give an idea about the content of the instance. For a video class, the thumbnail of the first cut is displayed.

Even though the composite icon browsing method is for many objects, the composite icon window cannot always represent all the retrieved objects altogether because of the screen size. For example, for classes *Student, Professor, Department,* and, *Course* respectively, the COMIB can present at most 30, 30, 72, and 72 default composite icons altogether in the normal composite icon window of Figure 5, and at most 104, 104, 338, and 338 default composite icons altogether in the maximized composite icon window. As the number of attributes in a composite icon path increases, the expressive power of composite icons increases, but the number of composite icons shown altogether decreases. Thus, as shown in Figure 5, the slide window is used for solving this problem partially by increasing the internal window size to the arbitrary size. But, if internal window size is greater than 4 times the shown window size, it cannot give the overview of objects effectively because of the limited capacity of the human memory.

### 4.2.1. *Navigation via Composite Icons with Schema Browsing*

"Navigation" is an iterative process in which a user scan an object, select one of its directly referred objects, and so on. It is very helpful for users who do not know what to look for or who do not know enough about the database. But, when there are too many objects, it is tedious for the user to repetitiously navigate through objects one by one, along the same path. Since a composite icon path associates composite icons with objects, it is possible for the user to easily inspect various kinds of composite icons from the given objects, by modifying the composite icon path. This gives users the effect of navigating through multimedia objects along the several paths of a class aggregation hierarchy. Consequently, it reduces the user's tedious work of repetitious short-sighted navigation.

In order to navigate through multimedia objects via composite icons, one needs only to add the navigation paths to the current composite icon path. Then the system automatically makes and presents composite icons according to the modified composite icon path. For example, while looking at the composite icons of student objects as shown in Figure 5, suppose a user wants to navigate through the advisors' pictures of all the given students. Then, by adding the nested attribute, 'advisor.picture' to the current composite icon path, {'name','picture'}, he can see more expressive composite icons including the advisor's picture as shown in the bottom left subwindow of Figure 6.

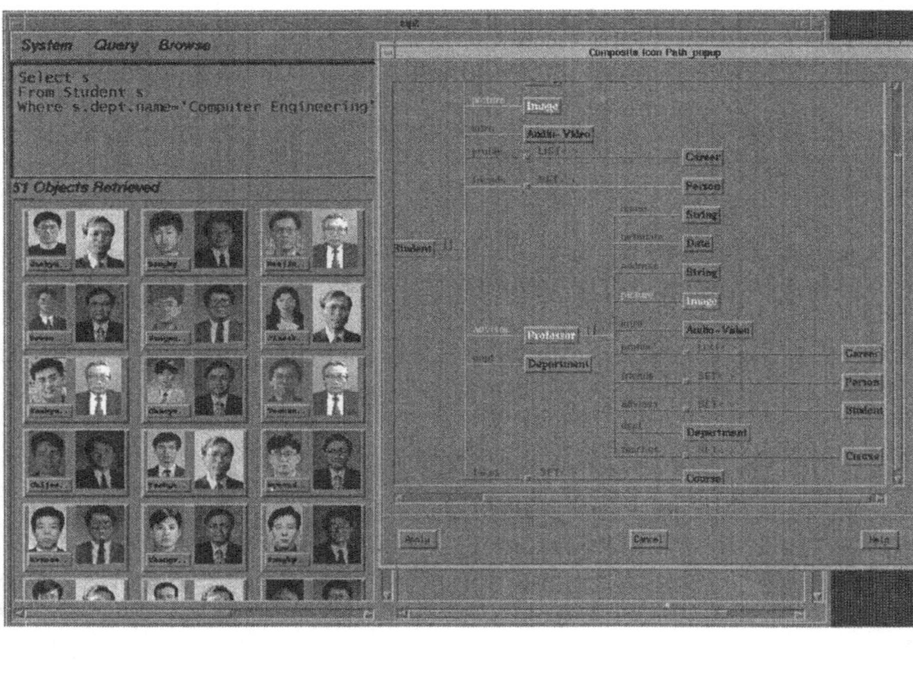


*Figure 6.* Navigation via Composite Icons

For a novice user who knows little about the aggregation hierarchy, COMIB helps him to directly manipulate the composite icon path on the visualized aggregation hierarchy of the query result. In order to represent the cylic navigation path that recursively traverses the aggregation hierarchy, the COMIB visualizes the aggregation hierarchy as a tree rather than a graph. The nodes represent the class and the edges represent the class-attribute relationships, i.e., the label, the source, and the destination of an edge represent the attribute name, the class that contains the attribute, and the domain class, respectively. Specially, the nodes corresponding to the attributes in the current composite icon path are highlighted on the tree. If a leaf node of the tree represents one of the user-defined classes, the node can be zoomed in interactively. And, while browsing and zooming in the tree, the user can toggle the leaf node as highlighted or not. Therefore users can easily understand the conceptual structure of the query result using the iterative refinements approach [2, 24], and can directly specify the composite icon path using a mouse.

For example, Figure 7(a), the composite icon path window of Figure 5, represents the aggregation hierarchy of class Student and the current composite icon path, {'name','picture'}. In order to add the attribute, 'advisor.picture' to the current composite icon path, first the user zooms in the leaf node, i.e. the attribute 'advisor' by additionally visualizing the aggregation hierarchy of the domain class, *Professor*. And he highlights the edge and the node representing the attribute, 'advisor.picture'. The enlarged aggregation hierarchy with the modified composite icon path, {'name', 'picture', 'advisor.picture'} is shown in Figure 7(b), the composite icon path window of Figure 6.

Therefore, without repetitious navigation, users can see objects and the referred objects at the same time by directly specifying the navigation paths in the current composite icon path with a mouse.

### *4.3. Step 3: Object Browsing*

To retrieve a multimedia object fully, users have to select the corresponding icon with the mouse. When selecting one composite icon in the bottom left subwindow, the multimedia object corresponding to the selected icon is retrieved. Objects are presented one at a time. For example, the right subwindow of Figure 8 presents the currently selected object of the class *Student*. This allows users to retrieve any object directly without scanning next or previous object repetitively.

When presenting an object, it is not easy to display its referred objects fully because of the limited space of the screen. Most DBMS browsers display these referred objects as the object names, OIDs, or the type names. On the other hand, the COMIB displays these referred objects as the default composite icon for a single-valued attribute, or the set of default composite icons for a multi-valued attribute. For example, intro, friends, advisor, dept, and takes attributes are presented according to the default composite icon path of the domain classes *Audio-Video*, *Person*, *Professor*, *Department*, and *Course* respectively. The enhanced expressiveness for the object enables users to understand the query result better.

In addition, any referred object can be fully presented in the new pop-up window by selecting the composite icon corresponding to the object. For example, as shown in Figure

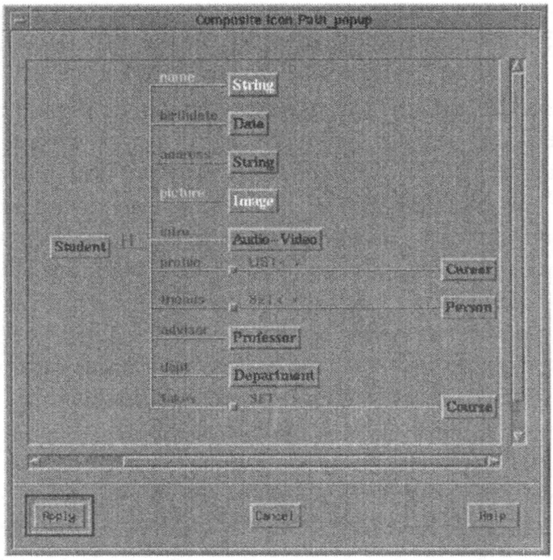


(a) original composite icon path: {'name','picture'}

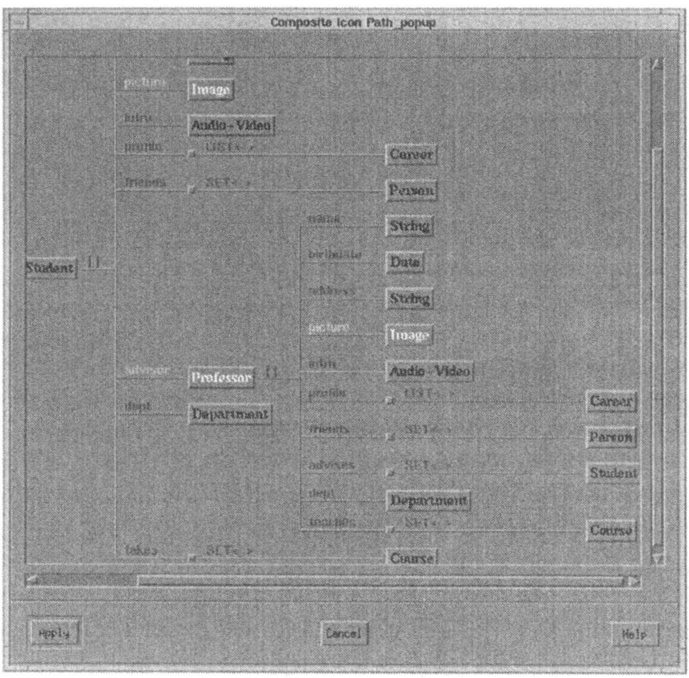


(b) modified composite icon path: {'name','picture','advisor.picture'}

*Figure 7.* Modification of Composite Icon Path

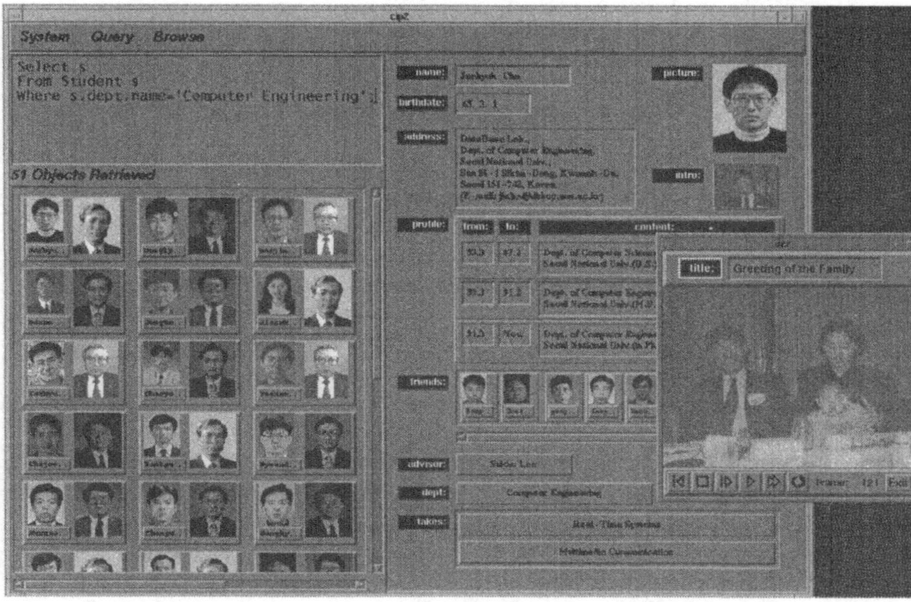


*Figure 8.* Presentation of Multimedia Objects

8, the object of *Audio-Video* class is presented by selecting the composite icon of intro attribute value.

## 5. A Mechanism of COMIB

COMIB allows users to perform the entire retrieval work according to the three execution steps using the four facilities; querying, composite icon browsing, schema browsing, and object browsing. We define all the basic objects and operations for this retrieval work first, and then describe the internals of and interactions between those steps with these objects and operations. This formalism describes the execution mechanism of COMIB clear and helps the modular design of COMIB.

### *5.1. Objects and Operations*

Since a retrieval session is performed in a window, we will denote a session as *w* and represent the information and actions of the entire retrieval session as objects and operations according to *w*. The objects for each session *w* are defined in Table 1.

In Table 2, the definitions of all the browsing operations of the COMIB are presented. These browsing operations are classified into operations transforming between objects and

| Objects | Role |
|---|---|
| *w* | *a retrieval session* |
| *query(w)* | *the query statement formulated by a user* |
| *result(w)* | *a set of retrieved objects as the query result* |
| *type(w)* | *the class name of an element object of result(w)* |
| *extent(T)* | *the extents of class T* |
| *current(w)* | *the object currently displayed in the window w at a moment* $current(w) \in result(w) \subseteq extent(type(w))$ |
| *cip(w)* | *the current composite icon path* |
| *defaultCIP(T)* | *the default composite icon path of class T* *specially, cip(w) is initialized as defaultCIP(type(w))* |
| *icon(w)* | *the data projected from result(w) according to cip(w)* *i.e., composite icons are thumbnail of icon(w)* |

*Table 1.* Objects for Retrieval

operations interacting with users. The former operations such as *executeQuery, elemType, makeIcon* are called the object operations and the latter operations such as *presentIcon, presentCIP, changeCIP, selectIcon, presentObject* are called the interface operations.

*T is the type of a retrieved object*
$T_{CIP}$ *is Set[Path], i.e.,* $\{p_1, p_2, \cdots, p_n\}$ *and* $p_i$ *is a path starting from T*
$T_{icon}$ *is the type of a composite icon*
$T_{window}$ *is the type of a window*

| | | | |
|---|---|---|---|
| *executeQuery( String )* | $\rightarrow$ | *Set[T]* | *// execute a query and return objects* |
| *elemType( Set[T] )* | $\rightarrow$ | *String* | *// return the class name of element object* |
| *makeIcon( Set[T],* $T_{CIP}$ *)* | $\rightarrow$ | $Set[T_{icon}]$ | *// return the composite icons from given objects* |
| *presentIcon(* $T_{window}, Set[T_{icon}]$ *)* | $\rightarrow$ | *Boolean* | *// present the composite icons* |
| *presentCIP(* $T_{window}, T_{CIP}$ *)* | $\rightarrow$ | *Boolean* | *// present the composite icon path as a tree* |
| *changeCIP(* $T_{window}$ *)* | $\rightarrow$ | $T_{CIP}$ | *// return the user's specification of composite icon path* |
| *selectIcon(* $T_{window}$ *)* | $\rightarrow$ | *T* | *// return the object corresponding to the selected icon* |
| *presentObject(* $T_{window}$*, T )* | $\rightarrow$ | *Boolean* | *// present the object* |

*Table 2.* Definitions of browsing operations

### *5.1.1. Object Operations*

The input arguments and the result of object operations are the objects to be used internally in the DBMS. The operation *executeQuery* sends to the DBMS the query formulated by a user, and returns the database objects. The operation *elemType* returns the element object type of the query result. These two operations are the basic application interface functions of the DBMS. The operation *makeIcon* returns a bag of objects that is projected from the query result according to the current composite icon path. This operation guarantees 1:1 mapping between the result set and the input set using the duplicate-allowing database operation *Project*.

---

***Function dividePath( s ):*** String $\mapsto$ { String }
  // divide s(input path string) into a set of path strings according to the set type
  // e.g.) "friends.name" $\rightarrow$ { ``friends'', ``name'' }
  *return* { $s_1, s_2, \cdots, s_l$ } ;
***End***

***Function getPathValue( x, $p_i$ ):*** T, String $\mapsto T_{basic}|T_{media}$
  *FG(x,y) is first(GetAttr(x,y))*
  *s := dividePath( $p_i$ ) ;*    /* $p_i \rightarrow \{s_1, s_2, \cdots, s_l\}$ */
  *return GetAttr(FG(* $\cdots FG(FG(x, s_1)), s_2) \cdots, s_{n-1})), s_l)$;
***End***

***makeIcon( so, p ):***
  *p is* { $p_1, p_2, \cdots, p_m$ } *where m is the number of paths in cip(w)*
    *return Project(so,* $\lambda y < (source, y)$,
    $(a_2, getPathValue(y, p_2))$,
    $\vdots$
    $(a_m, getPathValue(y, p_m)) >)$;
***End***

---

### *5.1.2. Interface Operations*

The interface operations create an object from the user's specification or present an existing object to users. Because these operations interact with users through the window, the working window object, *w* becomes the first input argument. The operation *presentIcon* presents the miniatures of the objects and the operation *presentCIP* visualizes the aggregation hierarchy and highlights the given composite icon path on this hierarchy. The operation *changeCIP* interacts with the user and then creates a new composite icon path. The operation *selectIcon* determines a currently selected icon and returns the corresponding object. The operation *presentObject* presents the given object according to the form-based presentation information. Within this presentation, the referred object is displayed as the corresponding composite icon.

---

***presentIcon( w, i ):***
  *i is* { $icon_1, icon_2, \cdots, icon_n$ } *where n is the number of objects*
  // calculate x, y, width, height for all pathes of *cip(w)*
  *for each* $icon_i$
    *for each path* $p_i$ *in cip(w)*
      *type := getType( type(w),* $p_i$ *);*

```
            switch( type ) {
                case String: // present the first 8 characters
                case Int:    // present the last 8 digits
                case Float:  // present the last 8 digits
                case Image:  // present the miniature of source image(default: 64x64)
                case Audio:  // present the first 7 seconds
                case Video:  // present the miniature of the first cut(default: 64x64)
            }
        // enroll the play callback for icon_i
End

presentCIP( w, cip ):
    // display the aggregation hierarchy of type(w)
    for each p_i in cip
        change the color of p_i as white
End

changeCIP( w ):
    s := { } ;
    while ( ( p_i := getMorePath( w ) ) is not null )
        addelement( p_i, s );
    return s;
End

selectIcon( w ):
    // get the selected icon icon from w
    return icon.source;
End

presentObject( w, o ):
    // get the presentation information of attributes of class type(o)
    for each attribute a_i of type(o)
        value := getAttr( o, a_i );
        switch( type( value ) ) {
            case String: // present value
            case Int: // present value
            case Float: // present value
            case Image: // present the image object(oid=value)
            case Audio: // present the object(oid=value)as the audio player button
            case Video: // present the object(oid=value)as the video player button
            case Tuple: presentObject( w, value );
            case Set: for each element object o_i in value
                            presentObject( w, o_i );
            case Object: // present the composite icon of value
        }
End
```

These browsing operations are applied to the objects of Table 1 for retrieval of the multi-media objects.

### *5.2. Interaction with COMIB*

A retrieval session can be pictorially described as shown in Figure 9, using the objects of Table 1 and the operations of Table 2. It shows the relationships between the objects and the operations. An object and an operation are represented as a node and an edge respectively. The vertical dashed line divides the operations into the object operations and the interface operations. And the horizontal dashed line divides a retrieval session into three steps, each of which consists of a group of objects and operations. We will show how a retrieval session is performed according to the execution steps.

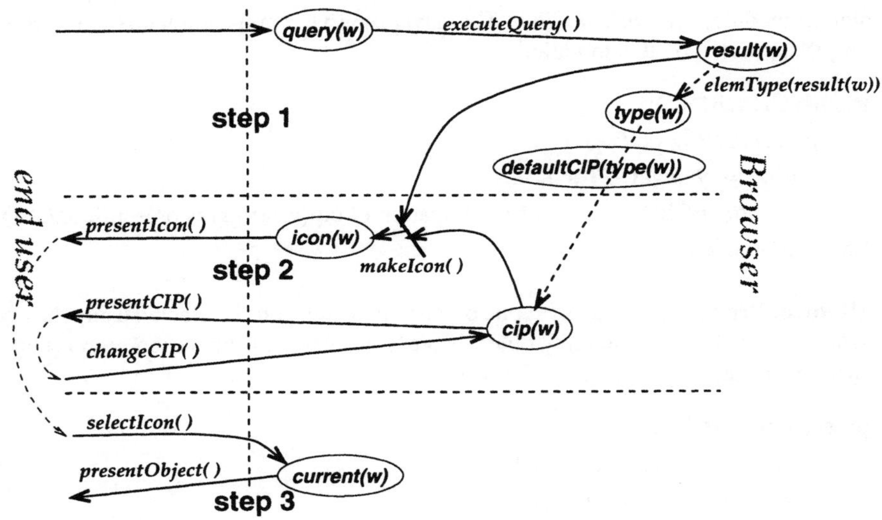


*Figure 9.* Execution flow of a Retrieval Session

**Step 1 (Querying):** First, the user performs the formulated query using operation *executeQuery* to get the query result. Internally the current composite icon path is initialized as the default composite icon path of the selected class to display the default composite icons from the beginning. This step of Figure 9 is described as follows:

1. ***executeQueryCB( ... ):***
2. *result(w) := executeQuery( query(w) );*
3. *type(w) := elemType( result(w) );*
4. *cip(w) := defaultCIP( type(w) );*
5. ***End***

**Step 2 (Composite Icon Browsing and Schema Browsing):** Composite icons corresponding to the objects are created using the operation *makeIcon* and displayed using the operation *presentIcon*. To present the object associated with the selected icon, *presentObjectCB()* is enrolled as the play callback of each icon. The module of presenting composite icons is described as follows:

```
presentIconCB( ... ):
        icon(w) := makeIcon( result(w), cip(w) );
        presentIcon( w, icon(w) );
         /* presentIcon() assigns presentObjectCB() to the play callback of each icon */
End pseudo-code
```

The selected attributes make up the current composite icon path using the operation *changeCIP*. Then, as shown in Figure 9, it automatically calls the above composite icon presentation module, *presentIconCB()*. The navigation via composite icons with schema browsing is supported by this module.

```
modifyCIPCB( ... ):
        presentCIP(w, cip(w));
        cip(w) := changeCIP( w );
        presentIconCB();          /* modification of cip(w) triggers presentIconCB() */
End pseudo-code
```

**Step 3 (Object Browsing):** Whenever one of the composite icons is selected using the operation *selectObject*, the corresponding object is presented using the operation *presentObject*. The object presentation module is as follows:

```
presentObjectCB( ... ):
        current(w) := selectIcon( w );
        presentObject( w, current(w) );
End pseudo-code
```

## 6. Implementation

COMIB is the core of the graphical user interface for the multimedia DBMS. It allows users to retrieve multimedia data easily. As shown in Figure 10, it uses some facilities of other tools such as the schema browser and the object presenter. The visual schema editor may visualize the schema and allow users to browse and manipulate the visualized schema directly. The schema browser in the visual schema editor is responsible for visualizing and browsing the schema. The object editor presents a multimedia object and allows users to directly edit the presented object. For presenting the composite icons and the objects, the object presenter in the object editor is used. Since the graphical user interface, not the DBMS kernel, supports the inheritance mechanism of BKEY as well as the management of presentation information, only the general OODBMS call-level interface is needed for the COMIB and other end-user tools. In other words, our end-user tools are loosely intergrated with an object-oriented multimedia DBMS ALPHA [10]. Therefore it is easy to adapt the COMIB to any object-oriented DBMS.

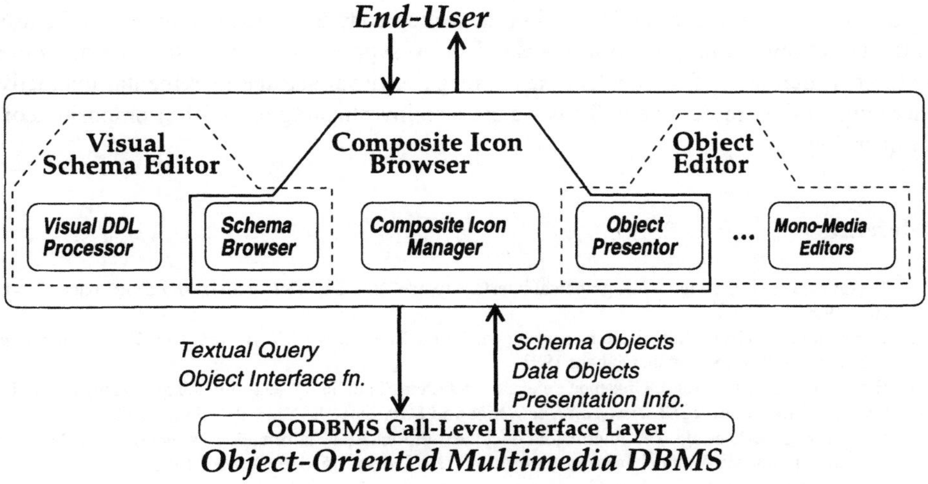


*Figure 10.* Architecture of COMIB

The prototype of COMIB was implemented using EuroBridge widgets and OSF/MOTIF widgets on top of the X window system. The full implementation is being developed in the C++ programming language on Sun SPARC workstations. It provides the functionality of presentation and minimization for each media such as image, audio, video. For video, the Berkeley MPEG decoder is used. For the synchronization of the audio and video, the MPEG video and audio player of the OGI's Distributed Systems Research Group is modified to directly access the database objects, and the modified version is used.

## 7. Conclusion

This paper describes the four facilities of COMIB (COMposite Icon Browser), namely querying, composite icon browsing, schema browsing, and object browsing, according to the three execution steps of a running example. The features of these facilities are as follows: 1) Querying controls the number of the objects to browse. 2) Composite icon browsing gives users the effects of browsing and navigating multimedia objects simultaneously in a screen using composite icons. 3) Schema Browsing aids the user to understand the conceptual structure of the information space. 4) Object Browsing enhances the object presentation form more expressively. We also showed how these features can overcome the three drawbacks of the browsing paradigm such as there being no overview of many objects, the repetitious short-sighted navigation, and the weak presentation of a multimedia object. In addition, we develop a formalism that explains an entire retrieval session, and describe implementation of COMIB based on this formalism.

We have concentrated on the browsing technique to overcome the three drawbacks. For the more seamless integration of querying and composite icon browsing, the use of composite icons for querying is needed. For example, the composite icons can be used in two ways for querying. First, icons can be used in the search condition. Second, icons can be used as the target objects in the From clause. But, to support these ways, that are addressed by the research area of the content-based image retrieval and the incremental interactive query proceesing, respectively. Thus we are also investigating use of the composite icons for querying.

## References

1. R. Agrawal et al. Odeview: The graphical interface to ode. In *Proc. of ACM SIGMOD Conf.*, pages 34–43, June 1990.
2. C. Batini et al. Visual strategies for querying databases. In *Proc. of IEEE Workshop on Visual Languages*, pages 183–189, Kobe, Japan, October 1991.
3. Elisa Bertino, Mauro Negri, Giuseppe Pelagatti, and Licia Sbattella. Object-oriented query languages: The notion and the issues. *IEEE Trans. on Knowledge and Data Eng.*, 4(3):223–237, June 1992.
4. S. Christodoulakis et al. The multimedia document presentation, information extraction, and document formation in minos: A model and a system. *ACM TOOIS*, 4(4):345–383, October 1986.
5. Stavros Christodoulakis and Leonidas Koveos. Multimedia information system: Issues and approaches. In Won Kim, editor, *Modern Database Systems*, chapter 4. ACM Press, 1995.
6. P. Constantopoulos et al. Multimedia document storage, classification and retrieval: Integrating the multos system. In *ESPRIT Conf. '89*, pages 819–836, 1989.
7. D. Fogg. Lessons from a 'living in a database' graphical query language. In *Proc. of ACM SIGMOD Conf.*, pages 100–106, Boston, MA, June 1984.
8. Michel Kuntz and Rainer Melchert. Ergonomic schema design and browsing with more semantics in the pasta-3 interface for e-r dbms. In *Proc. of Int'l. Conf. on E-R approach*, pages 419–433, Toronto, Canada, October 1989.
9. J.A Larson. A visual approach to browsing in a database environment. *IEEE Computer*, June 1986.
10. Sukho Lee et al. Design and implementation of the multimedia dbms alpha. *Journal of Korean Information Science Society*, 21(7):1181–1188, July 1994. In Korean.
11. M.K. Leong et al. Towards a visual language for an object-oriented multimedia database system. In T.L. Kunii, editor, *Visual Database Systems*. North Holland, 1989.
12. J.D. Mackinlay, G.G. Robertson, and S.K. Card. The perspective wall: Detail and context smoothly integrated. In *CHI '91 Proc.*, pages 173–179, April 1991.
13. Frank Manola. An evaluation of object-oriented dbms developments 1994 edition. Technical Report TR-0263-08-94-165, GTE Lab. Inc., 1994.
14. A. Motro. Browsing in a loosely structured database. In *Proc. of ACM SIGMOD Conf.*, pages 197–207, June 1984.
15. A. Motro et al. The design of KIVIEW: An object-oriented browser. In *Proc. of 2nd Int'l Conf. on Expert Database Systems*, pages 17–31, April 1988.
16. O2 Technology. *O2Tools Manual*, March 1995.
17. G.G. Robertson, J.D. Mackinlay, and S.K. Card. Cone trees: Animated 3d visualization of hierarchical information. In *CHI '91 Proc.*, pages 189–194, April 1991.
18. P. Rosengren et al. A tools oriented visual interface for multimedia databases. In *Proc. of Int'l Symp. on Next Generation Database Systems and Their Applications*, pages 219–226, Fukuoka, Japan, September 1993.
19. M. Sarkar and M.H. Brown. Graphical fisheye views of graphs. In *CHI '91 Proc.*, pages 83–91, Monterey, CA, May 1992.

20. B. Shneiderman. Tree visualization with tree-maps: A 2-d space filling approach. *ACM Transactions on Graphics*, 11(1):1–39, January. 1992.
21. Yoshinobu Tonomura and Shinji Abe. Content oriented visual interface using video icons for visual database systems. In *1989 IEEE Workshop on Visual Language*, pages 68–73, 1989.
22. UniSQL, Inc. *UniSQL/4GE Visual Editor User's Guide Release 3*, January 1995.
23. D. Woelk et al. Multimedia Applications and Database Requirements. In *Proc. of IEEE Symp. on Office Automation*, April 1987.
24. H. K. T. Wong and I. Kuo. GUIDE: Graphical user interface for database exploration. In *Proc. of Int'l. Conf. on Very Large Data Bases*, pages 22–32, Mexico City, Mexico, September 1982.
25. R.V. Zoeller and D.K. Barry. Dynamic self-configuring methods for graphical presentation of ODBMS objects. In *Proc. of 8th Intl. Conf. on Data Engineering*, pages 136–143, 1992.

**Jaehyuk Cha** received his B.S. degree in computer science and statistics, and his M.S. degree in Computer Engineering from Seoul National University, Seoul, Korea, in 1987 and 1991, respectively. He is currently a Ph.D. student in the Department of Computer Engineering at Seoul National University. His current research interests include database systems, multimedia systems, and distributed systems.

**Sukho Lee** received his B.A. degree in Political Science and Diplomacy from Yonsei University, Seoul, Korea, in 1964 and his MS and PhD in Computer Sciences from the University of Texas at Austin in 1975 and 1979, respectively. He is currently a professor of the Dept of Computer Engineering, Seoul National University, Seoul, Korea, where he has been leading the Database Research Laboratory. He has served as the president of Korea Information Science Society. His research interests include database management systems, multimedia database systems, and object-oriented database systems.

Multimedia Tools and Applications 3, 225–244 (1996)


# A Fractal-Based Clustering Approach in Large Visual Database Systems

AIDONG ZHANG azhang@cs.buffalo.edu
BIAO CHENG
*Department of Computer Science, State University of New York at Buffalo, Buffalo, NY 14260*

RAJ ACHARYA
*Department of Electrical and Computer Engineering, State University of New York at Buffalo, Buffalo, NY 14260*

**Abstract.** Large visual database systems require effective and efficient ways of indexing and accessing visual data on the basis of content. In this process, significant features must first be extracted from image data in their pixel format. These features must then be classified and indexed to assist efficient access to image content. With the large volume of visual data stored in a visual database, image classification is a critical step to achieve efficient indexing and retrieval. In this paper, we investigate an effective approach to the clustering of image data based on the technique of fractal image coding, a method first introduced in conjunction with fractal image compression technique. A joint fractal coding technique, applicable to pairs of images, is used to determine the degree of their similarity. Images in a visual database can be categorized in clusters on the basis of their similarity to a set of iconic images. Classification metrics are proposed for the measurement of the extent of similarity among images. By experimenting on a large set of texture and natural images, we demonstrate the applicability of these metrics and the proposed clustering technique to various visual database applications.

**Keywords:** content-based image retrieval, fractal coding, image clustering, texture and image database systems

## 1. Introduction

While large visual information systems require effective and efficient means of indexing and accessing images based on their content, research toward achieving this goal is still in a preliminary stage. Methods for indexing and accessing alphanumeric data in traditional databases are, in contrast, well understood. In these databases, categorization of data is straightforward on the basis of their semantics. Efficient data access can be supported by B-trees and other data structures. However, such traditional approaches to indexing may not be appropriate in the context of content-based visual data retrieval [1, 2, 6, 10, 13, 19, 28, 31]. In this context, visual queries are posed via visual or pictorial examples. A typical visual query might entail the location of all images in a database that contain a subimage similar to a given query image. Such a query could, for example, be used in a medical image setting to find an anomaly, such as a tumor, in a diagnostic image.

Generic tools are not currently available with which to accurately define image content. The automatic categorization and retrieval of images on the basis of content thus pose significant difficulties. Given the large volume of image data collected in a visual database, a manual approach to detecting and classifying images is both highly inefficient and prone to errors arising from subjective interpretation. Thus, the ability to automatically cluster images on the basis of content assumes a critical role on supporting efficient indexing. To efficiently handle retrieval on a large volume of images, these images must be first classified into various categories before indexing on image content features are performed. The clustering of images into categories on the basis of content is thus a prerequisite to the effective and efficient execution of visual queries.

An approach which has drawn much recent attention involves the extraction of the texture features of images from their mathematical representations used in various image compression techniques. Texture is an important underlying primitive in human visual perception, including coarseness, contrast, and directionality [18, 27, 31]. These texture characteristics can be used to support content-based image retrieval. Recent developments in the field of image data transformation and compression provide an interesting approach to describing the content of image texture. Image data transformation and compression eliminate data redundancy by decorrelating the pixel values of image data. The resulting transformed data represents the salient characteristics of the image, and these can be used to perform image retrieval. Among the image compression methods, JPEG [30], wavelet transformation [12], and fractal coding [3, 9, 14, 23] have recently drawn much attention. It has been demonstrated that both the Discrete Cosine Transform (DCT) used in JPEG and wavelet transformation can be used for texture classification and discrimination [24, 25]. Fractal image compression, a compacted mathematical representation of image data, also offers a promising approach to the description of the texture features of image data. Initial research in this direction [23, 32–34] has demonstrated that fractal coding of image data can be used to recognize useful texture features which can assist content-based image retrieval.

In this paper, we investigate a technique for efficient clustering of images in a large visual database. Using this clustering technique, a clustering tool can be built to assist the automatic categorization of images in a large visual database on the basis of their similarity to a set of iconic images. Indexing strategies should then be designed on image feature vectors in each category. Through this clustering strategy, efficient retrieval of visual data based on their content can be supported.

The proposed clustering approach is developed based on the extension of fractal image representation. In this approach, the technique of fractal coding is applied to image clustering through its extension to *joint fractal coding* between images. This approach, applicable to pairs of images, can be used to determine the degree of their similarity. Images in a visual database can be categorized in clusters on the basis of their similarity to a set of iconic images. Classification metrics are proposed for the measurement of the extent of similarity among images. This process operates automatically, with no human assistance required to determine the points of similarity between images. The proposed clustering technique is well-suited to incorporation into many digital library applications. A generic clustering tool has been developed which can be used in various visual database applications.

The rest of the paper is organized as follows. Section 2 discusses the main characteristics of fractal coding for image compression and its potential on image clustering. In Section 3, we propose the joint fractal coding technique which can be used to support image clustering. Section 4 introduces similarity measuring metrics to determine the degree of similarity between images. Experimental results of clustering on natural images will also be presented.

In Section 5, we discuss the relationship between clustering and indexing. Other potential clustering approaches are also considered. Concluding remarks and directions for future research are offered in Section 6.

## 2. Background

In this section, we will first provide an introduction to the technique of fractal image compression, and then discuss the central role to be played by fractal-based similarity comparison in content-based image clustering.

### 2.1. *Fractal-based image compression*

Fractal image compression is based on the mathematical results of iterated function systems (IFS) [20]. Barnsley and Sloan [3] first recognized the potential of IFS for computer graphics applications. The formal mathematical description of IFS can be found in [7]. Jacquin [14, 15] proposed a fully automated algorithm for fractal image compression. Informally, fractal image compression partitions an image into a collection of non-overlapping regions, termed *ranges*. For each such image range, the fractal encoder finds a larger block within the same image (termed the domain block, $D$) such that a transformation $w(D)$ of this block is the best approximation of the range block, according to an appropriate criterion of similarity. The *fractal code* for the range consists of the geometrical positions of the range and domain as well as the transformation. While the pixel data contained in the range and in the domain are used to determine the fractal code, they are not part of the code itself. As the transformations are much more compactly represented than the pixel data, a high compression ratio can be achieved [7]. Principally, this approach assumes that image redundancy can be captured and exploited through piecewise self-similarity transformations [15]. The original image can be approximated from a finite number of iterations of its fractal code.

We now provide implementation details to explain this compression technique. We assume that the image partition is generated by a quadtree scheme [7]. In this scheme, images are partitioned into square range blocks. For each range block, we select a domain block with twice the range size and then average groups of $2 \times 2$ pixels to get a reduced block with the same number of pixels as the range. Let a reduced block $D_j$ and the range $R_i$ contain $n$ pixel intensities $a_1, \ldots, a_n$ and $b_1, \ldots, b_n$, respectively. We use the rms (root mean square) metric to compare the distance between $D_j$ and $R_i$. The rms distance $\text{Dist}_i$ between $D_j$ and $R_i$ is computed as follows:

$$\text{Dist}_i = \sqrt{\frac{\sum_{k=1}^{n}(s_i \times a_k + o_i - b_k)^2}{n}} \tag{1}$$

where $s_i$ and $o_i$ are values which minimize $\text{Dist}_i$ defined in Formula (1) for the given $a_k$, $b_k$ ($k = 1, \ldots, n$). This will provide us contrast and brightness settings that make the affinely transformed $a_k$ values have the least squared distance from the $b_k$ values. Details on the calculations of $s_i$ and $o_i$ can be found in [7]. Out of the possible domain blocks, a domain

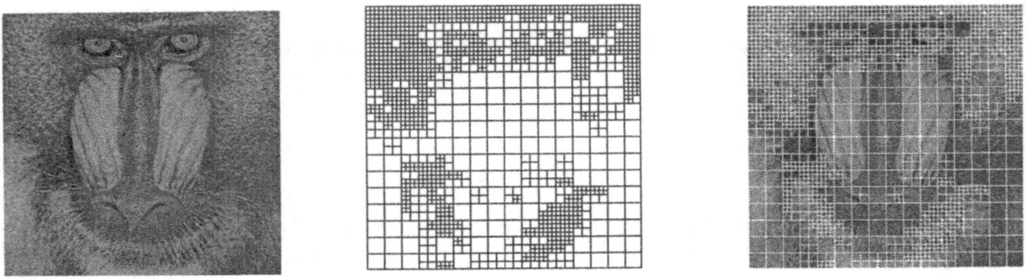

(a) (b) (c)

*Figure 1.* (a) Original image; (b) range partitions of the image; (c) range partitions over the original image.

block with a distance below the tolerance level[1] (Computed by Formula (1)) will be selected as the best approximated transformation of $R_i$. In formulating the transformation for $R_i$ based on its best domain block, there are two spatial dimensions and the grey level adds a third dimension. Thus, the transformation $w_i$ for the range $R_i$ is a combination of a geometrical transformation as well as luminance transformation. In matrix form, $w_i$ can be expressed as follows:

$$w_i \begin{bmatrix} x \\ y \\ z \end{bmatrix} = \begin{bmatrix} a_i & b_i & 0 \\ c_i & d_i & 0 \\ 0 & 0 & s_i \end{bmatrix} \begin{bmatrix} x \\ y \\ z \end{bmatrix} + \begin{bmatrix} e_i \\ f_i \\ o_i \end{bmatrix} \tag{2}$$

where $z$ denotes the pixel intensity at position $(x, y)$, $s_i$ is the contrast scaling, and $o_i$ is the luminance offset.

To regenerate the original image, only the transformation and the positions of the range and domain need to be transmitted to the decoder. The fractal code of the image, iteratively applied to any initial image, will generate a simulated version of the original image. To ensure convergence at the decoder, the union of all transformations for the whole image must be contractive. Fractal image compression is lossy [11].

Since Jacquin's initial work on fractal image coding, many extensions have been proposed to enhance the initial concept. Worthy of mention is the introduction by Fisher et al. [8] of adaptive methods in the encoding process. They proposed the use of quad-tree, rectangular, and triangular partitions of the range blocks to improve image fidelity. Other researchers have focused on reducing the complexity of encoding or increasing decoding speed [16].

Figure 1 illustrates a range partitioning of an image. As shown in figure 1(b), the range partitioning of the image closely approximates the original image.

### 2.2. *Observations*

The fractal image compression approach exploits self-similarity within the image to compact the image data. As pointed out in [7], most naturally occurring images can be compressed by taking advantage of this type of self-similarity. We observed that the strategy of using self-similarity to compact image data proposed in the fractal image compression can be extended to perform the similarity comparison between images.

Consider a range $R_i$ and its domain $D_j$ in an image $\mathcal{M}_1$. The distance $\text{Dist}_i$ between $R_i$ and the reduced block of $D_j$ through averaging pixels offers a similarity measure between the two blocks within a given tolerance. Consider another image $\mathcal{M}_2$. We can determine whether or not there exists a block $D'_j$ within $\mathcal{M}_2$ which can be used to perform the same function as that of $D_j$, that is, to best simulate $R_i$ within a given tolerance. If there exists such a block, we then have one of the following situations:

- $\mathcal{M}_2$ has a subimage that is also a subimage in $\mathcal{M}_1$ which contains both $R_i$ and $D_j$; or
- $\mathcal{M}_2$ has a block which contains texture that is similar to $R_i$ in $\mathcal{M}_1$ within a given tolerance.

Note that, in the second situation given above, the degree of similarity between $R_i$ in $\mathcal{M}_1$ and the domain $D'_j$ selected from $\mathcal{M}_2$ is measured through affine transformation of $D'_j$ to $R_i$. The affine transformation through averaging pixels takes into account noise and distortion that might appear in images.

Applying these observations, we introduce a clustering approach to classifying images on the basis of their texture similarity in the following section.

## 3. Fractal-based clustering

In this section, we will present a fractal-based clustering approach to the classification of a large visual database. We will first introduce a joint fractal coding approach between images and then discuss the application of this approach to the clustering of images.

### 3.1. *Joint fractal coding*

Let $\mathcal{M}_1$ and $\mathcal{M}_2$ be two images. Based on the observations given in Section 2.2, the similarity between two images $\mathcal{M}_1$ and $\mathcal{M}_2$ can be identified by performing the fractal coding of $\mathcal{M}_1$ using both $\mathcal{M}_1$ and $\mathcal{M}_2$. The fractal encoder approximates the ranges of $\mathcal{M}_1$ by domains that lie within both $\mathcal{M}_1$ and $\mathcal{M}_2$. The similarity in texture between a portion of $\mathcal{M}_1$ and a portion of $\mathcal{M}_2$ will then likely result in a range in the former being best approximated by a domain in the latter. If the two images are closely related according to a given metric, we could then select many similar features from $\mathcal{M}_2$ rather than from $\mathcal{M}_1$ in the formulation of the contractive transformations of $\mathcal{M}_1$. The similarity of the two images can thus be assessed by noting the frequent choice of a domain block in $\mathcal{M}_2$ as the best transformed domain for a range in $\mathcal{M}_1$.

We shall now define a *joint fractal coding* procedure between images. Let $\mathcal{M}_1$ and $\mathcal{M}_2$ be two images. $\mathcal{M}_1$ is partitioned into $4 \times 4$ size-fixed square range blocks. The domain size is fixed at $8 \times 8$ square blocks. The joint fractal coding of $\mathcal{M}_1$ with respect to $\mathcal{M}_2$ indicates that, during the process of fractal coding for each range block $R_i$ in $\mathcal{M}_1$, the joint fractal coding procedure seeks the best approximated domain block for $R_i$ in both $\mathcal{M}_1$ and $\mathcal{M}_2$. If the two images are similar in texture, the best domain block for $R_i$ could be found in $\mathcal{M}_2$ rather than in $\mathcal{M}_1$. Let $\text{Dist}_{1i}$ denote the minimum rms distance between $R_i$ and its domain block found within $\mathcal{M}_1$ and $\text{Dist}_{2i}$ denote the minimum rms distance between $R_i$ and its domain block found within $\mathcal{M}_2$. Let $\epsilon > 0$ be a given tolerance level for determining the closeness between $\mathcal{M}_1$ and $\mathcal{M}_2$. If the formula below holds:

$$|\text{Dist}_{1i} - \text{Dist}_{2i}| < \epsilon, \tag{3}$$

we then choose the domain block in $\mathcal{M}_2$ as the best approximation domain block of $R_i$.

A domain block in either $\mathcal{M}_1$ or $\mathcal{M}_2$ that is the minimum rms distance from the range block is selected. We term such domains that are chosen from $\mathcal{M}_2$ *joint domains*. Assume that the domain blocks in $\mathcal{M}_2$ always have higher selection priority than those in $\mathcal{M}_1$. Clearly, if $\mathcal{M}_1$ and $\mathcal{M}_2$ are closely related in texture, many domain blocks from $\mathcal{M}_2$ might then, following the selected criterion, be chosen.

The joint fractal coding technique provides a robust approach to clustering images. Given an image database and a set of iconic images, the images in the database can be categorized in clusters on the basis of their similarity to the iconic images. This procedure can be accomplished as follows. For each iconic image, the joint fractal coding procedure approximates the ranges of the iconic image by domains that lie within both itself and each database image. The number of domains that are chosen from each database image for the iconic image can then be obtained. The similarity of the iconic image and the database image can then be assessed by noting the frequent choice of a block in the database image as the domain for the iconic image. Thus, this number plays an important role on determining the similarity between the iconic and the database images. Detailed discussion on similarity measurement will be given in Section 4.

Note that the joint fractal coding approach is time-consuming. Thus, to apply the proposed image clustering technique in visual databases, one should use this image clustering technique to categorize database images off-line on the basis of a set of iconic images.

### 3.2. *Experiments*

We will now present the experimental results conducted for the joint fractal coding of images. A testbed of the image database has been constructed from Brodatz texture images and their mixed variants [5]. Subimages were selected from Brodatz texture image set and used as iconic images. For the experimental results presented in this context, we have set the size of the iconic image at $32 \times 32$ pixels and the database image size at $96 \times 96$ pixels.

Figure 2 presents five iconic images, each of which is associated with three similar database images. Table 1 presents the results of experiments involving joint fractal coding between each iconic image and each database image given in figure 2. These results indicate that, for a given iconic image, a majority of matching domain blocks can be found in a similar database image, while relatively few matching domain blocks can be found in a non-similar database image. Let the joint domain block selection rate be the ratio of the number of domains found in the database image to the total number of range blocks in the icon. Consider iconic image Icon(a). Domain blocks for this image were found in similar images B004j, B004k, and B004l at the joint domain block selection rates of 78.12%, 90.62%, and 90.62%, respectively. However, domain blocks were found in non-similar images B034b,

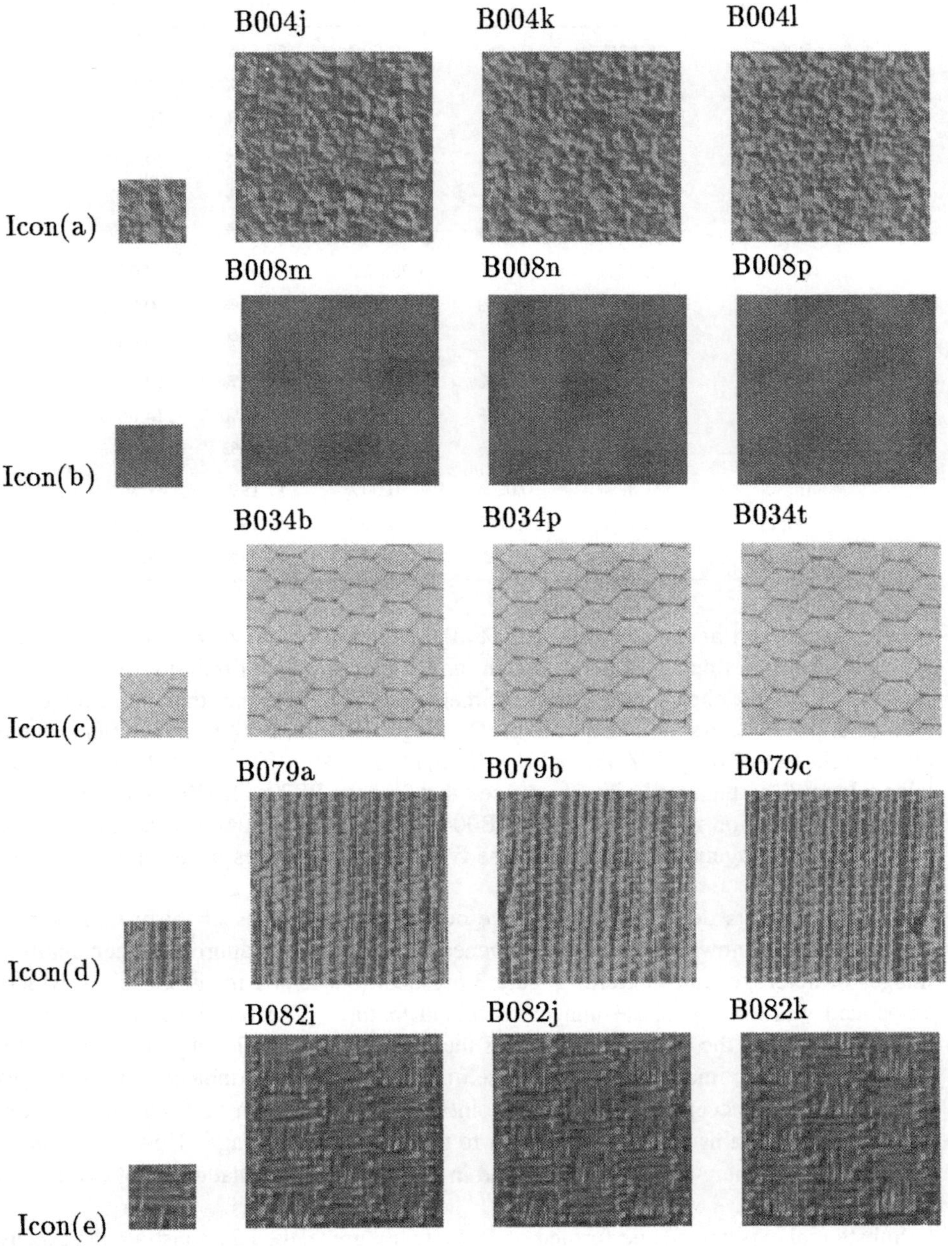


*Figure 2.* Iconic and database images from Brodatz album.

*Table 1.* Similarity comparison between images.

| Test image | Icon(a) | Icon(b) | Icon(c) | Icon(d) | Icon(e) |
|---|---|---|---|---|---|
| B004j | **78.12%** | 0.00% | 0.00% | 65.62% | 45.31% |
| B004k | **90.62%** | 0.00% | 0.00% | 67.19% | 37.50% |
| B004l | **90.62%** | 0.00% | 0.00% | 70.31% | 26.56% |
| B008m | 10.94% | **60.94%** | 0.00% | 15.62% | 39.06% |
| B008n | 7.81% | **51.56%** | 0.00% | 7.81% | 21.88% |
| B008p | 17.19% | **75.00%** | 0.00% | 15.62% | 43.75% |
| B034b | 0.00% | 0.00% | **90.62%** | 0.00% | 0.00% |
| B034p | 0.00% | 0.00% | **85.94%** | 0.00% | 0.00% |
| B034t | 1.56% | 0.00% | **100.00%** | 0.00% | 0.00% |
| B079a | 39.56% | 0.00% | 0.00% | **75.00%** | 12.50% |
| B079b | 39.06% | 0.00% | 0.00% | **71.88%** | 14.06% |
| B079c | 53.12% | 0.00% | 0.00% | **85.94%** | 14.06% |
| B082i | 21.88% | 0.00% | 0.00% | 17.19% | **87.50%** |
| B082j | 18.75% | 3.12% | 0.00% | 17.19% | **87.50%** |
| B082k | 28.12% | 1.56% | 0.00% | 18.75% | **89.06%** |

B034p, and B034t at rates of only 0.00%, 0.00%, and 1.56%, respectively. Note that, although database images B008m, B008n, and B008p are also dissimilar to Icon(a), the joint domain block chosen rates for these images are slightly higher than those for B034b, B034p, and B034t. As indicated in figure 2, images B008m, B008n, and B008p are more closely related to B004j, B004k, and B004l than to B034b, B034p, and B034t. Similarly, taking Icon(d) as the iconic image, we see that images B079a, B079b, and B079c have the highest selection rates, with images B004j, B004k, and B004l also having relatively high rates. This again indicates that these two groups of images have somewhat similar texture.

The experiments described above were conducted on images of fairly homogeneous texture. We shall now discuss the effectiveness of the proposed approach when applied to images of heterogeneous texture. Figure 3 presents four iconic images, each of which is associated with five database images of mixed texture. The matching rate under each database image in the figure demonstrates the experimental results of joint fractal coding between the iconic image and the database image. These results indicate that, for a given iconic image, an acceptable number of joint domain blocks can be found in a database image which contains a subimage similar to the given iconic image. However, relatively few matching domain blocks will be found in a database image that does not contain such a subimage.

Substantial experiments performed on Brodatz texture testbed demonstrate the potential of applying the joint fractal coding approach to the classification of large volume of visual data based on their content similarities. Several similarity metrics need be identified to be used for such a purpose. We will discuss these issues in the next section.

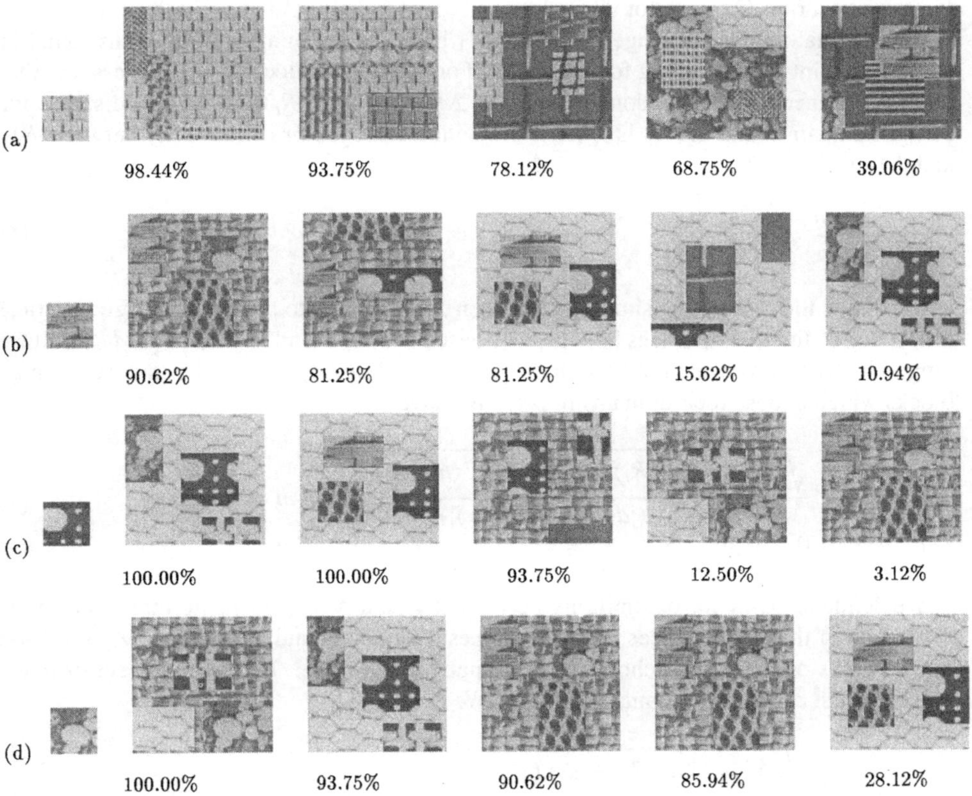


*Figure 3.* Iconic images and database images with mixed texture.

## 4. Similarity measurement for classifying visual data

In this section, we will develop the parameters that can be used to provide effective similarity measurement on a large visual database. In such an environment, generic similarity measurement is necessary to classify various types of natural images.

### *4.1. Similarity metrics*

In the process of joint fractal coding between images $\mathcal{M}_1$ and $\mathcal{M}_2$ discussed in Section 3.1, the number of joint domains selected from $\mathcal{M}_2$ is an important factor in determining whether $\mathcal{M}_2$ is similar to $\mathcal{M}_1$. Additionally, the degree of the minimum rms distance plays an important role. If the number of joint domains selected from $\mathcal{M}_2$ is relatively small but the average minimum rms distance between range blocks and the corresponding transformed domain blocks is fairly low, we may still consider the two images to be similar. The similarity rate between $\mathcal{M}_1$ and $\mathcal{M}_2$ should thus be determined based on several factors including the number of domains found in $\mathcal{M}_2$ for $\mathcal{M}_1$ and the average difference between the minimum rms distances for those domain blocks found in $\mathcal{M}_1$ itself and in $\mathcal{M}_2$.

Let the total number of range blocks in $\mathcal{M}_1$ be $n$ and the number of domains found in $\mathcal{M}_2$ using joint fractal coding for $\mathcal{M}_1$ be $m$. For each range block $R_i$ in $\mathcal{M}_1$, assume that the rms distance for the best domain found in $\mathcal{M}_1$ itself is $d_1(R_i)$ and the rms distance for the best domain found in $\mathcal{M}_2$ is $d_2(R_i)$. We define the *A-factor* of similarity between $\mathcal{M}_1$ and $\mathcal{M}_2$ as follows:

$$A = \frac{m}{n}. \tag{4}$$

We define the *B-factor* of similarity between $\mathcal{M}_1$ and $\mathcal{M}_2$ to be the normalized average difference of the rms distances between the best domains found in $\mathcal{M}_1$ and $\mathcal{M}_2$ for those range blocks of $\mathcal{M}_1$ which choose their domains within $\mathcal{M}_1$. Let $S_1$ be the set of range blocks which choose their domains in $\mathcal{M}_1$. We have

$$B = \begin{cases} \dfrac{\sqrt{\left(\sum_{R_i \in S_1} (d_1(R_i) - d_2(R_i))^2\right) / (n - m)}}{\max_{R_i \in S_1} (|d_1(R_i) - d_2(R_i)|)} & \text{if } m \neq n, \\ 0 & \text{if } m = n. \end{cases} \tag{5}$$

We define the *C-factor* of similarity between $\mathcal{M}_1$ and $\mathcal{M}_2$ to be the normalized average difference of the rms distances between the best domains found in $\mathcal{M}_1$ and $\mathcal{M}_2$ for those range blocks of $\mathcal{M}_1$ which choose their domains within $\mathcal{M}_2$. Let $S_2$ be the set of range blocks which choose their domains in $\mathcal{M}_2$. We have

$$C = \begin{cases} \dfrac{\sqrt{\left(\sum_{R_i \in S_2} (d_1(R_i) - d_2(R_i))^2\right) / m}}{\max_{R_i \in S_2} (|d_1(R_i) - d_2(R_i)|)} & \text{if } m \neq 0, \\ 0 & \text{if } m = 0. \end{cases} \tag{6}$$

As $m$ in (4) is always less than or equal to $n$ and both $B$ in (5) and $C$ in (6) are normalized to be between 0 and 1, all three similarity factors $A$, $B$, and $C$ are in the range of [0, 1].

We now discuss the calculation of the similarity rate between the two images. Informally, if $A$ is large, then we can assume that many domains in $\mathcal{M}_2$ are similar to $\mathcal{M}_1$. Thus, the similarity rate between the two images should be high. $B$ has negative effect on the similarity rate. If $B$ is large, then the best approximated domains are found within $\mathcal{M}_1$ in a high degree. As a result, the similarity rate between $\mathcal{M}_1$ and $\mathcal{M}_2$ should be relatively low. In contrast, $C$ has positive effect on the similarity rate.

Let *alpha, beta, and gamma* (denoted $\alpha$, $\beta$, and $\gamma$, respectively) be weighting parameters. We propose the following formula to calculate the similarity rate between images:

$$\text{Sim Rate} = \alpha \times A + \beta \times (1 - B) + \gamma \times C, \tag{7}$$

where $\alpha$, $\beta$ and $\gamma$ ($0 \leq \alpha, \beta, \gamma \leq 1$ and $\alpha + \beta + \gamma = 1$) are the parameters that determine the weight of participating factors in the similarity rate.

The choices of parameters $\alpha$, $\beta$, $\gamma$ should be decided based on the nature of applications. We choose a set of images from Brodatz Collect [5] as our sample image database. These images are divided into groups according to selected iconic images, with each group having 10 similar images to its iconic image.

The experiments include the following steps: (1) calculate the values of $A$, $B$, and $C$ for each iconic image and a database image; (2) given different parameters $\alpha$, $\beta$ and $\gamma$, calculate the similarity rate for each pair of an iconic image and a database image; (3) for each iconic image, select the top 10 database images with highest similarity rates. We then evaluate the retrieval effectiveness in terms of precision [29]. As stated in [26], precision is the ratio of the number of relevant images retrieved to that of all the images retrieved. More formally, if $A$ is the set of relevant images in database and $B$ is the set of retrieved images, then precision is calculated by the conditional probability: precision $= P(A \mid B)$. In our experiments, we use:

$$\text{precision} = \frac{\text{Retrieved\_relevant}}{\text{Total\_retrieved}}. \tag{8}$$

In figure 4, for icon Icon001, we see that the highest precision is 80% when $\alpha$ reaches 0.6 or higher and $\beta$ and $\gamma$ are any numbers satisfying $\alpha + \beta + \gamma = 1$ and $0 \leq \beta, \gamma \leq 1$. This suggests the importance of the number of domains found in the database image should be emphasized. For Icon006, we see that when the value of $\alpha$ is in the range of [0.5, 0.8] and $\beta$ is in the range of [0.0, 0.1], the precision reaches the highest number possible. For Icon054, we see that when $\alpha$ is in the range of [0.5, 1.0] and $\beta$ is in [0.0, 0.5], the precision reaches the highest number possible. For Icon065, when $\alpha$ is in the range [0.4, 0.7], the precision reaches the highest.

Following a large volume of experiments conducted on various values of $\alpha$, $\beta$, and $\gamma$, the results indicate that $\alpha$ is the most important factor among the three parameters and should be set in the range of [0.5, 1.0], $\beta$ should be chosen below 0.2, and $\gamma$ should also be under 0.3. Specific values for the parameters should be decided empirically.

### 4.2. *Icon-based clustering*

We have conducted comprehensive experiments on visual data clustering based on the approach and similarity metrics given above. A testbed of the image database has been constructed from the VisTex image database obtained from the MIT media lab. Iconic images are randomly selected from image cuts. For the experimental results presented in this context, we have set the size of the iconic image at $32 \times 32$ pixels and the database image size at $128 \times 128$ pixels.

We now present four sets of experiments on the similarity between icons and database images. In the first set, we choose $\alpha$, $\beta$, and $\gamma$ to be 0.7, 0.2, and 0.1, respectively. For the icon given in figure 5(a), the clustering techniques and similarity measurement were tested on the VisTex database. Figure 5(b) illustrates 10 database images and their similarity rates based on Formula (7).

As can be observed from figure 5, the similarity rates between the database images and the icon tend to decrease as the features of the database images get less similar to that of the given icon. In fact, all "building" images with similar design features to the icon are

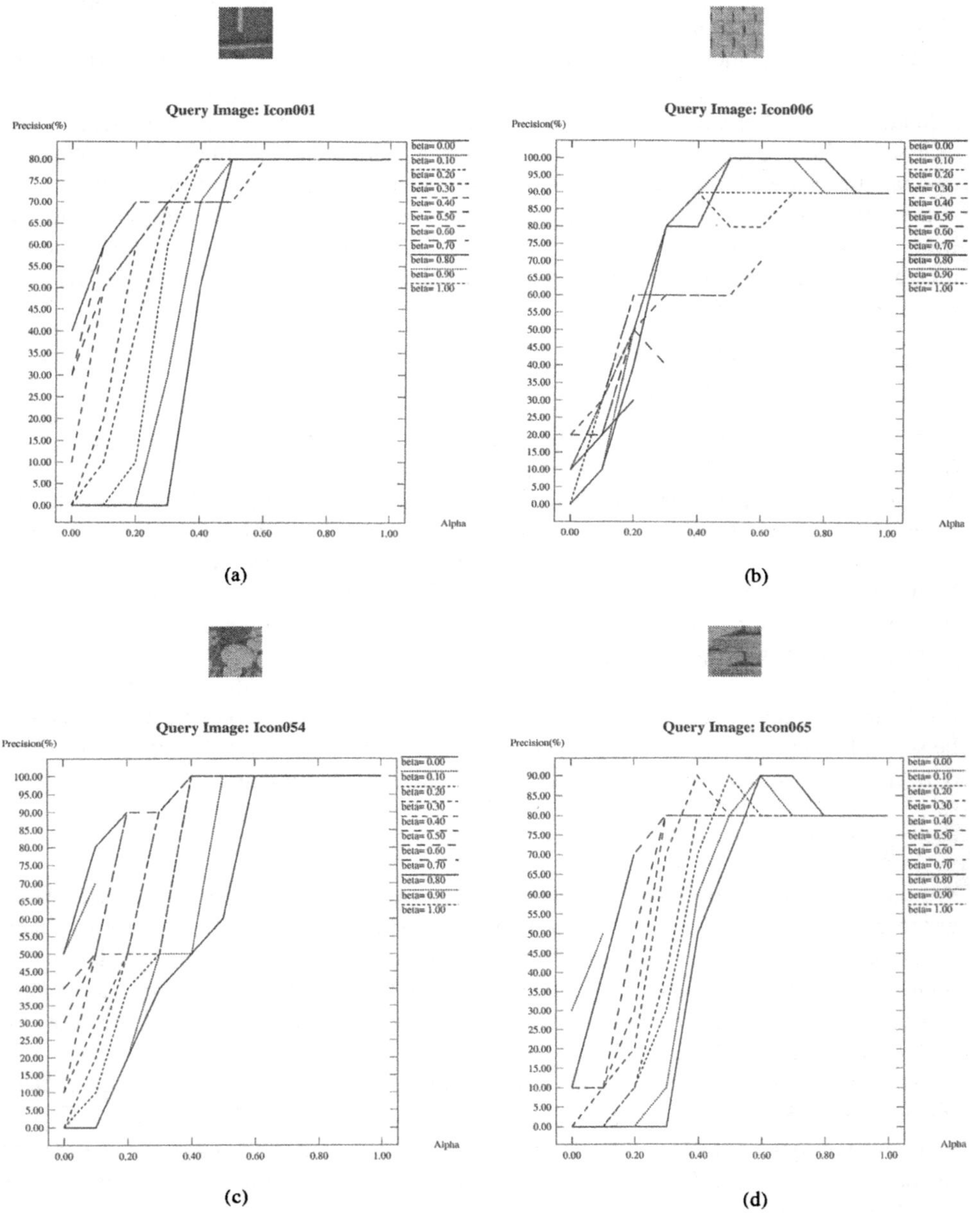


*Figure 4*. Retrieval precision and parameters for similarity measure.

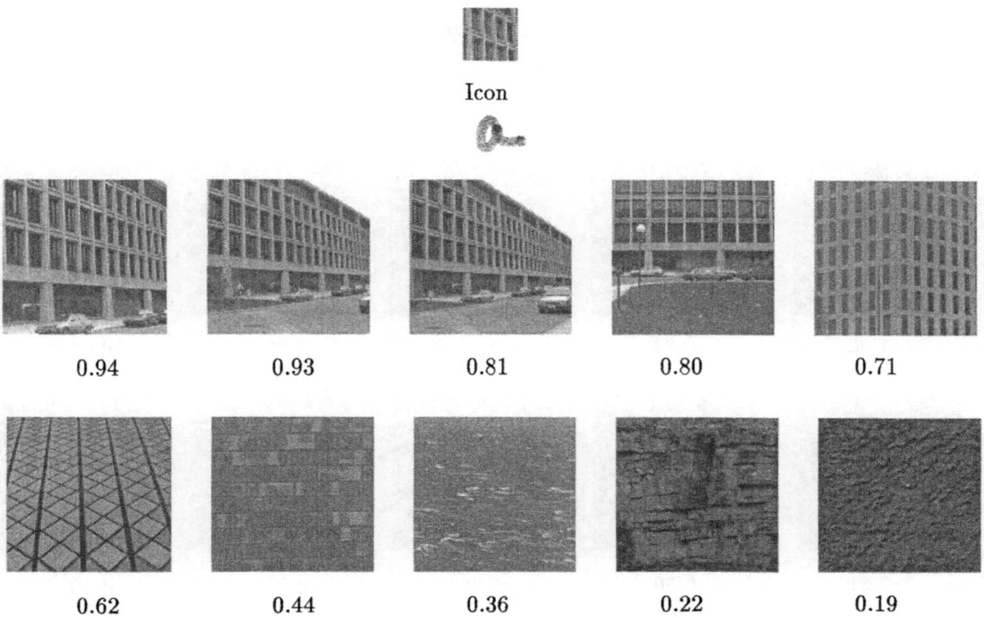


(b)

*Figure 5.* VisTex database images clustering.

identified at top similarity rates. Images containing "tiles" do contain some similar features to the given icon, but the image containing "sand" has few features similar to the given icon and thus, similarity rate is only 0.19, which is at the lowest.

For the second set of experiments, we choose $\alpha$, $\beta$, and $\gamma$ to be 1.0, 0.0, and 0.0, respectively. For the icon given in figure 6(a), the clustering techniques and similarity measurement were tested on the VisTex database. Figure 6(b) illustrates 10 database images and their similarity rates based on Formula (7).

Similar to the first set of experiments, as can be observed from figure 6, the similarity rates tend to decrease as the features of database images get less similar to that of the given icon. Also, all "water" images with similar design features to the icon are identified at top similarity rates.

For the third set of experiments, we choose $\alpha$, $\beta$, and $\gamma$ to be 0.6, 0.2, and 0.2, respectively. For the icon given in figure 7(a), the clustering techniques and similarity measurement were tested on the VisTex database. Figure 7(b) illustrates 10 database images and their similarity rates based on Formula (7).

As also can be observed from figure 7, the similarity rates tend to decrease as the features of database images get less similar to that of the given icon. Also, all images with similar design features to the icon are identified at top similarity rates.

For the fourth set of experiments, we choose $\alpha$, $\beta$, and $\gamma$ to be 1.0, 0.0, and 0.0, respectively. For the icon given in figure 8(a), the clustering techniques and similarity measurement were tested on the VisTex database. Figure 8(b) illustrates 10 database images and their similarity rates based on Formula (7).

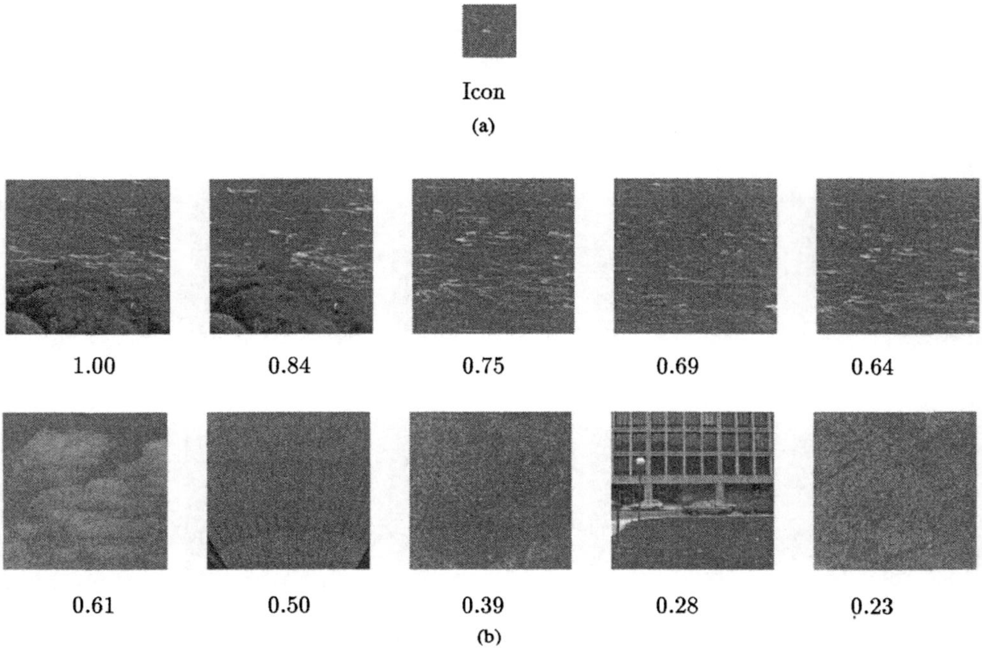


*Figure 6.* VisTex database images clustering.

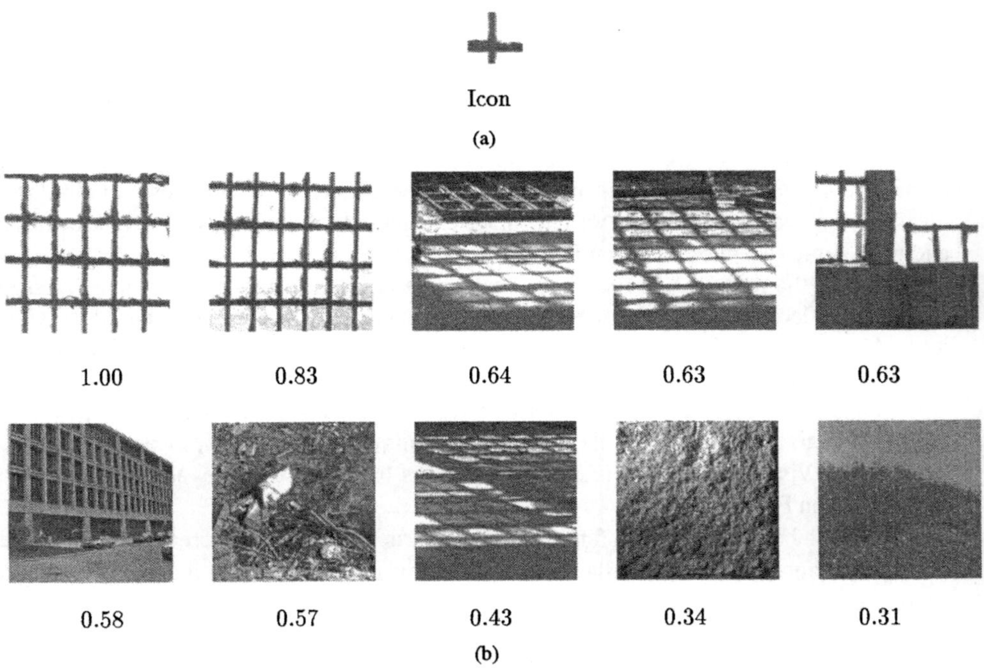


*Figure 7.* VisTex database images clustering.

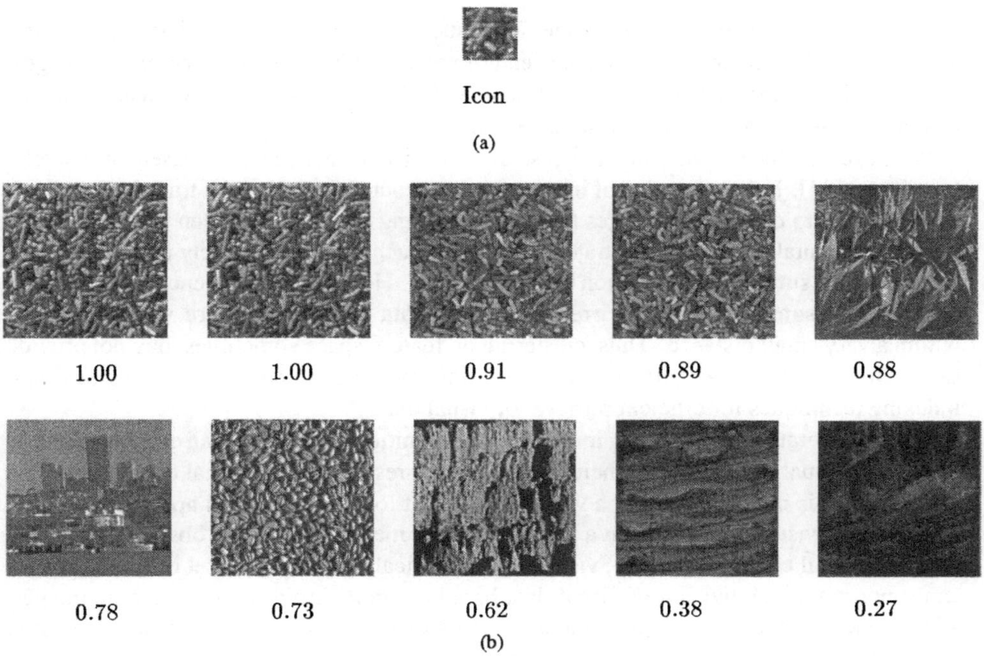


*Figure 8.* VisTex database images clustering.

As can be observed from figure 8, the similarity rates tend to decrease as the features of database images get less similar to that of the given icon. Also, all images with similar design features to the icon are identified at top similarity rates.

Based on these experimental results, we can see that visual data can be categorized into different degrees of similarity groups based on their similarity rates to a given icon. Usually, both high and medium degrees of similarity groups would be significant for supporting content-based visual data retrieval. For our experimental needs, we classify visual data into three categories: high similarity group (similarity rate $\geq 0.7$), medium similarity group (similarity rate is between 0.69 and 0.4), and low similarity group (similarity rate is less than 0.39). Note that an image may belong to several groups for different icons.

## 5. Discussion

In this section, we discuss the relationship between clustering and indexing. Other potential clustering approaches are also considered.

### *5.1. Clustering and indexing*

Substantial research has been directed toward the support of efficient indexing techniques based on feature vectors of images [2, 4, 14, 21, 22, 25]. The feature vector of an image represents various features of the image. Most successful approaches are based on texture, shape, and color features to formulate feature vectors. Given feature vectors of images, indexing algorithms such as R*-tree, $R^+$-tree, and TV-tree [4, 14, 22] have been proposed to support efficient accesses to visual databases.

We have conducted experimental research on visual data retrieval based on wavelet transforms [34]. Feature vectors of images are constructed from wavelet transforms, which are then used to distinguish images through measuring distances between feature vectors. Our experimental results demonstrate that this approach can be effectively used to perform content-based similarity comparison between images. However, we also encounter a critical problem that some semantically irrelevant visual data may have feature vectors that fall within a very small distance. Thus, clustering on feature space sometimes may not provide satisfactory solutions. A more effective clustering approach is needed to be integrated into indexing techniques for efficient retrieval of visual data.

The incorporation of clustering into indexing techniques can provide an effective method to classify visual data based on their similarity features. In a large visual database, such a classification is not intended to be very accurate but to provide a good approximate categorization of visual data based on a given similarity measurement. We observe that, using the joint fractal coding technique, visual data classification based on a set of iconic images can support a novel division of visual data based on their similarity to the iconic images. Within each category of images, feature vectors of images can then be generated using the techniques proposed in several image retrieval approaches based on color, texture, and shape [2, 21, 26]. A novel indexing technique can be selected from various existing indexing techniques that are the variations of R-tree [4, 14, 22]. These indexing techniques can be applied to the feature vectors of images. A *hierarchical index structure* can then be established for the entire visual database. Firstly, a variation of R-tree is used to construct an index on the selected icons. Secondly, the clustering approach given above is applied to classify the visual data based on the given icons. Thirdly, the variation of R-tree technique is used again on each cluster to construct an index on the images within each cluster. An efficient visual data retrieval system will then be established based on these tools.

The proposed clustering and indexing approach can efficiently support visual queries. For a given visual database, we establish a hierarchical index structure based on a set of selected icons. The selection of such icons is application-oriented. For a given query image, the retrieval will first be performed on the iconic images by comparing the distance of feature vectors between the query image and icons. A subset of the iconic images will be identified as the subdirectories for further retrieval. For a large visual database, this step can substantially narrow the search to more relevant images. The query can then be more efficiently performed on the selected clusters. As visual data are classified into different degrees of groups, some degree of similarity retrieval can be supported by search similar images from different groups.

### 5.2. *Other clustering approaches*

One advantage of the proposed clustering approach is that the self-similarity found within the image is used as a threshold indicator for the degree of the similarity between blocks in different images. Such a similarity threshold is automatically adjusted to suit the individual blocks under consideration. Experimental results have demonstrated that this approach is highly effective.

Other clustering approaches are possible. For example, similarity matching between icons and database images can be performed using their JPEG coefficients or rms calculations with identically-sized ranges and domains. However, similarity threshold selection in these instances poses significant problems. Since the similarity between images in a pixel format has not been clearly defined, it becomes difficult to appropriately designate thresholds for the ranges within each icon which will result in the selection of the proper domains. These issues merit more detailed discussion than can be pursued in this paper.

## 6. Conclusion and future research

In this paper, we have presented approaches to the clustering of image data based on the fractal image coding. A hierarchical clustering and indexing structure can be designed for large visual databases. The proposed image clustering approach uses a joint fractal coding technique between images, which can be used to determine the degree of their similarity. As we have shown in our experimental results, the self-transformation property of fractal image compression offers the opportunity to compact image data, and this property can also be utilized to identify the similarity between images. This process operates automatically, with no human assistance required to extract image content for retrieval. Thus, the proposed approach is especially important to large visual database applications.

Initial experimental results conducted on natural images have demonstrated this approach to be highly effective. Additional research and experimental work must be done to efficiently incorporate these techniques into domain specific visual database and digital library applications. A comprehensive clustering system for large visual databases can be effectively developed.

## Note

1. Encodings made with lower tolerance will have better fidelity, and those with higher tolerance will have worse fidelity [7].

## References

1. M. Arya, W. Cody, C. Faloutsos, J. Richardson, and A. Toga, "QBISM: A prototype 3-D medical image database system," IEEE Data Engineering Bulletin, Vol. 16, No. 1, pp. 38–42, 1993.
2. J.R. Bach, S. Paul, and R. Jain, "A visual information management system for the interactive retrieval of faces," IEEE Transactions on Knowledge and Data Engineering, Vol. 5, No. 4, pp. 619–628, 1993.
3. M.F. Barnsley and A.D. Sloan, "A better way to compress images," BYTE, pp. 215–223, 1988.
4. N. Beckmann, H.P. Kriegel, R. Schneider, and B. Seeger, "The R*-tree: An efficient and robust access method for points and rectangles," in Proceedings of ACM-SIGMOD International Conference on Management of Data, Atlantic City, NJ, May 1990, pp. 322–331.

5. P. Brodatz, Textures: A Photographic Album for Artists and Designers, Dover: New York, 1966.
6. S.K. Chang, C.W. Yan, D.C. Dimitroff, and T. Arndt, "An intelligent image database system," IEEE Transaction on Software Engineering, Vol. 14, No. 5, pp. 681–688, May 1988.
7. Y. Fisher, Fractal Imaging Compression: Theory and Applications, Springer-Verlag, 1995.
8. Y. Fisher, E.W. Jacobs, and R.D. Boss, "Iterated transformation image compression," Technical Report TR-1408, Naval Oceans Systems Center, San Diego, CA, 1991.
9. Y. Fisher and A.F. Lawrance, "Fractal image compression for mass storage applications," SPIE Image Storage and Retrieval Systems, 1662, 1992.
10. T. Gevers and A.W.M. Smeulders, An Approach to Image Retrieval for Image Databases, Vol. 720, Lecture Notes in Computer Science, Springer-Verlag: Berlin.
11. M. Gharavi-Alkhansari and T.S. Huang, "Fractal-based techniques for a generalized image coding method," in Proceedings IEEE ICIP, 1994.
12. M.L. Hilton, B.D. Jawerth, and A. Sengupta, "Compressing still and moving images with wavelets," Multimedia Systems, Vol. 2, No. 5, pp. 218–227, Dec. 1994.
13. T.-Y. Hou, P. Liu, A. Hsu, and M.-Y. Chiu, "Medical image retrieval by spatial features," in IEEE Conference on Systems, Man, and Cybernetics, 1992.
14. A.E. Jacquin, "Image coding based on a fractal theory of iterated contractive image transformations," IEEE Transactions on Image Processing, Vol. 1, No. 1, 1992.
15. A.E. Jacquin, "Fractal image coding: A review," Proceedings of the IEEE, 1993, Vol. 81, No. 10.
16. S. Lepsqy, G.E. Olen, and T.A. Ramstad, "Attractor image compression with a fast non-iterative decoding algorithm," in Proceedings of ICASSP-93, 1994.
17. K.-I. Lin, H.V. Jagadish, and C. Faloutsos, "The TV-tree: An index structure for high-dimentional data," The VLDB Journal, Vol. 3, No. 4, pp. 517–542, Oct. 1994.
18. W. Niblack, R. Barker, W. Equitz, M. Flickner, E. Glasman, D. Petkovic, P. Yanker, C. Faloutsos, and G. Taubin, "The qbic project: Querying images by content using color, texture, and shape," Technical report, IBM Technical Report, 1993.
19. F. Rabitti and P. Savino, "Automatic image indexation and retrieval," in Conference on Intelligent Text and Image Handling, 1991.
20. D. Saupe and R. Hamzaoui, "A guided tour of the fractal image compression literature," in ACM SIGGRAPH'94 Course Notes, New Directions for Fractal Modelling in Computer Graphics, July 1994.
21. M.F.H. Sawhney, W. Niblack, J. Ashley, Q. Huang, B. Dom, M. Gorkani, J. Hafner, D. Lee, D. Petkovic, D. Steele, and P. Yanker, "Query by image and video content: The QBIC system," IEEE Computer, Vol. 28, No. 9, 1995.
22. T. Sellis, N. Roussopoulos, and C. Faloutsos, "The $R^+$-tree: A dynamic index of multidimensional objects," in Proceedings of the 18th VLDB Conference, 1987.
23. A.D. Sloan, "Retrieving database contents by image recognition: New fractal power," Advanced Imaging, Vol. 9, No. 5, pp. 26–30, 1994.
24. J.R. Smith and S. Chang, "Transform features for texture classification and discrimination in large image databases," in Proceedings IEEE ICIP, 1994.
25. J.R. Smith and S.-F. Chang, "Quad-tree segmentation for texture-based image query," in Proceedings of ACM Multimedia 94, San Francisco, California, Oct. 1994, pp. 279–286.
26. J.R. Smith and S.-F. Chang, "Automatic image retrieval using color and texture," Technical report, Columbia University, 1995.
27. H. Tamura, S. Mori, and T. Yamawaki, "Texture features corresponding to visual perception," IEEE Transactions on Systems, Man, and Cybernetics, Vol. 8, No. 6, June 1978.
28. A. Turtur, F. Prampolini, M. Fantini, R. Guarda, and M.A. Imperato, "IDB: An image database system," IBM Journal of Research and Development, Vol. 35, No. 1, pp. 88–96, Jan. 1991.
29. C.J. van Rijsbergen, Retrieval Effectiveness, in K.S. Jones (Ed.), Information Retrieval Experiment, Butterworths, 1981, pp. 32–43.
30. G.K. Wallace, "The JPEG still picture compression standard," Communications of the ACM, Vol. 34, No. 4, pp. 30–44, 1991.
31. J.K. Wu and A.D. Narasimhalu, "Identifying faces using multiple retrievals," IEEE Multimedia, Vol. 1, No. 2, pp. 27–38, 1994.

32. A. Zhang, B. Cheng, and R. Acharya, "Texture-based image retrieval in image database systems," in Procceedings of the Sixth International Workshop on Database and Expert Systems Applications (DEXA), London, United Kingdom, Sept. 1995. Invited paper.
33. A. Zhang, B. Cheng, and R. Acharya, "An approach to query-by-texture in image database systems," in Proceedings of the SPIE Conference on Digital Image Storage and Archiving Systems, Philadelphia, Oct. 1995.
34. A. Zhang, B. Cheng, R. Acharya, and R. Menon, "Comparison of wavelet transforms and fractal coding in texture-based image retrieval," in Proceedings of the SPIE Conference on Visual Data Exploration and Analysis III, San Jose, Jan. 1996.

**Aidong Zhang** received her Ph.D. degree in computer science from Purdue University, West Lafayette, Indiana, in 1994. She is currently an assistant professor in the Department of Computer Science at State University of New York at Buffalo. Her current research interests include transaction and workflow management, distributed database systems, multimedia database systems, educational digital libraries, and content-based image retrieval. She is a member of the IEEE Computer Society, ACM, and ACM SIGMOD.

**Biao Cheng** received his B.S. in Computer Science from Wuhan University, China in 1986 and his Master in Engineering from the Institute of Automation, Chinese Academy of Sciences in Beijing, China in 1989, and his M.S. and Ph.D. in Computer Science from the State University of New York at Buffalo in 1993 and 1996 respectively. His research interests include Multimedia Database Systems, Image/Video Processing and Retrieval, Distributed Database Systems and Internet Applications Development.

**Raj Acharya** obtained his Ph.D. from the University of Minnesota/Mayo Graduate School of Medicine in 1984. He worked with the Dynamic Spatial Reconstructor project at Mayo Clinic (1981–85). During 1984–1986, he was a research scientist at GE-CGR in Paris, France. He is currently an Associate Professor of Electrical and Computer Engineering at SUNY-Buffalo and the Director of Biomedical Imaging Group. He is on the editorial board of the Journal of Computerized Medical Imaging and Graphics. He was General Chair of SPIE Conference on Biomedical Image Processing (1992 and 1993). He is currently General Chair of 1994 SPIE International Conference on Physiology and Function from Multidimensional Images. He was also Cochair of 1994 IEEE Workshop in Biomedical Image Analysis. His research interests are in Image Processing and Multimedia Computing.

Multimedia Tools and Applications 3, 245–267 (1996)


# Content-Based Retrieval for Trademark Registration

J.K. WU jiankang@iss.nus.sg
C.P. LAM prong@iss.nus.sg
B.M. MEHTRE, Y.J. GAO AND A. DESAI NARASIMHALU
*Institute of Systems Science, National University of Singapore, Kent Ridge, Singapore 0511, Republic of Singapore*

**Abstract.** With ever increasing number of registered trademarks, the task of trademark office is becoming increasingly difficult to ensure the uniqueness of all trademarks registered. Trademarks are complex patterns consisting of various image and text patterns, called *device-mark* and *word-in-mark* respectively. Due to the diversity and complexity of image patterns occurring in trademarks, due to multi-lingual word-in-mark, there is no very successful computerized operating trademark registration system. We have tackled key technical issues: multiple feature extraction methods to capture the shape, similarity of multi-lingual word-in-mark, matching device mark interpretation using fuzzy thesaurus, and fusion of multiple feature measures for conflict trademark retrieval. A prototype System for Trademark Archival and Registration (STAR) has been developed. The initial test run has been conducted using 3000 trademarks, and the results have shown satisfaction to trademark officers and specialists.

**Keywords:** content-based retrieval, image database, trademark registration, evaluation of content-based retrieval system, shape features

## 1. Introduction

Due to advances in imaging technologies and retrieval methods, many new applications involving image information retrieval are emerging. For example, object recognition using content-based retrieval has been demonstrated by Grosky and Mehrotra [9] and Wu et al. [21], Bach et al. [3] utilized visual routines for both insertion and retrieval. Petrakis and Orphanoudakis [14] developed a methodology for retrieving of medical images based on spatial relationships and properties of objects. Pentland et al. [13] described a photobook system, which is a set of interactive tools for browsing and searching images for face, shape, and texture. Kato proposed a TRADEMARK system [12], which allows design and similarity-retrieval of trademark-like graphics patterns [12]. A Computer-Aided Facial Image Inference and Retrieval system (CAFIIR) has been developed in the Institute of Systems Science (ISS), National University of Singapore, which provides four special image data access methods, namely, visual browsing, similarity retrieval, fuzzy retrieval, and free text retrieval, for criminal identification [22].

Trademarks can be as simple as consisting of a few characters and as complex as having both text and image of certain complexity. Some trademark image design is influenced by modern art and hence the images are near impossible for description. Retrieval of trademarks using associated text description cannot work. Due to diversity and complexity of trademark images, it is very difficult to capture its visual properties such as shape, structure and complexity. Multiple and sophisticated feature extraction methods should be developed. Trademark protection is world wide and the words in the trademarks are multilingual. This increases the difficulty of searching conflict trademarks in a large database.

Due to technical difficulties, there is little work done on trademark registration system. Because of the uniqueness of trademark retrieval, the above mentioned image database techniques cannot apply. We have tackled the trademark retrieval problem by using a set of real trademarks. We have developed a special similarity measures for multi-lingual word-in-mark, proposed multiple feature extraction methods, introduced fuzzy thesaurus for matching concepts, designed a combined retrieval strategy. Some of these techniques were discussed in our previous paper [23]. We will report our new results in the following sections.

Based on these technical research results, our prototype System for Trademark Archival and Registration (STAR) now has passed its initial test. The system is developed using our Content-based Retrieval Engine for multimedia information system (CORE). In the following sections, Section 2 describes color segmentation method used for trademarks, feature extraction methods are discussed in Section 3, the retrieval scheme is presented in Section 4, evaluation and learning of similarity measures is in Section 5, and experimental results and discussion are in the final sections.

## 2. Representation of trademarks

Among the technical difficulties in implementing automated search of trademarks are the following: an unlimited variety of symbolic patterns, multi-lingual words, unlimited abbreviations, styled characters, importance of meaning of the words (rather than appearance), abstract graphics. All these variations can occur singly or in any combination of the above. We use structural classification of trademarks as shown in figure 1.

Trademarks are represented as structural patterns consisting of word-in-mark and device-mark. The word-in-mark is text, and the device-mark is graphic or image. The structural classification can be illustrated by 12 trademark images of airline companies shown in figure 2. Trademark image "INTERFLUG" (3,2) has word-in-mark only. Trademark images (1,1), (1,2), (1,3), (3,3), and (4,1) have device mark only. Image (4,2) can be

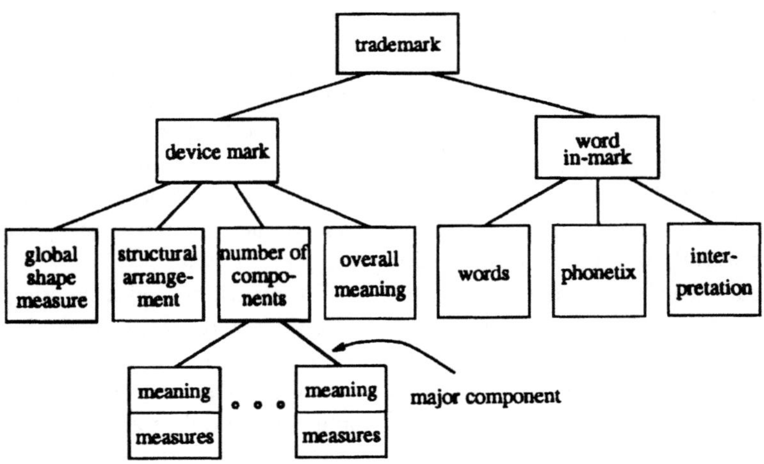


*Figure 1.* Structural representation of trademarks.

*Figure 2.* Trademarks of some Airline Companies. We use row and column number to label these trademark images. For example, Finnair will be labeled as (1,3) image.

considered as device mark, as character "M", is not just a character but has graphics. It looks like a crown with a potential for conflict with trademark (1,2). Trademark images (2,1), (3,1) have both word-in-mark and device mark.

According to trademark registration rules, word-in-mark similarity will be considered in three aspects: word-in-mark text, phonetics, and interpretation. The device-mark is either a graphic or an image object. Styled characters are also considered as graphics, such as "M" in image (4,2) in figure 2. Most device-marks consist of several components. To describe their shape or texture, we need to separate them by segmentation process.

The description of a graphic or image device involves the shape/texture description of components and the spatial relationship between components. For example, trademark image (3,3) in figure 2 has two components. The component "circle" contains the component "leaf". Or in the other words, the components "leaf" is within the component "circle". In the device-mark of trademark image (3,1) in figure 2, there are four components. The spatial relationships among these four components can be described in many ways. To avoid the complexity of spatial relationship description in the retrieval, we choose to describe device mark structures by *outline/background shape* and *component grouping*. This will be discussed further in the next section.

Most device-marks of trademarks carry particular meaning. For example, image (4, 1) is an eagle. When searching for similar trademarks, the meaning of device-marks is weighted quite high. For example, both image (1, 2) and (4, 2) in figure 2 have the meaning "crown". They are similar in meaning even though they are totally different as far as structure and shape are concerned. Of course, structure and shape are also important when computing the similarity. In case the device-mark does not have a particular meaning, then structure, shape, and texture measures are the only factors used to evaluate the similarity value. This is true, for example, for the trademark shown in (3, 1) of figure 2.

## 3. Segmentation of trademarks

Segmentation of trademark is the first step for trademark archival. At this step, the user needs to enter the trademark particulars (owner, date of application, etc.), enter word-in-mark and identify major graphic component. Since the nature of trademark images is very complex and lacks any commonality, fully automatic segmentation is almost impossible. Hence, we have adopted a semi-automatic and interactive segmentation.

A partial automatic segmentation is performed by labeling the components using color segmentation technique [17], and the result is presented to the user, through an interactive user interface. The results of such a segmentation are presented in different colors for different components for easy identification (or grouping) by the user. The user-interface facilitates grouping of one or more components together. Once a component or a group of components is selected by the user, they are extracted and highlighted. The image feature measures are then computed.

Figure 3 shows the interface panel of segmentation module. On the left side of the window there are function buttons for loading trademark image, filling in trademark particulars, etc. User can choose to activate button "Word-In-Mark", "Device-Mark", or "Composite Mark" depending on the type of the trademark loaded. A trademark image which is loaded will be displayed in the centre (on the right side of the function buttons). If the word-in-mark is in English, its phonetics will be derived automatically, otherwise user needs to type in phonetics. The device mark panel appears when either "Device-Mark" or "Composite Mark" button is activated. The buttons on the first row are used to specify certain aspects of the device mark: Component grouping captures the structural information of the device mark. This indicates spatial arrangement of the components of trademark (e.g., triangular, rectangular, circular, star, concentric, parallel, symmetric). The meaning of a component is contained in a small dictionary, on which a fuzzy thesaurus is built. Optionally, a component can be designated as major (important) component, when there are more than one components. Buttons in the second row provide functions to select components and compute feature measures. In case of composite trademarks like the one shown in figure 3, the device mark is too small for feature extraction. In such cases full sized (or an enlarged version) image will be loaded by activating the "Aux-Image" button.

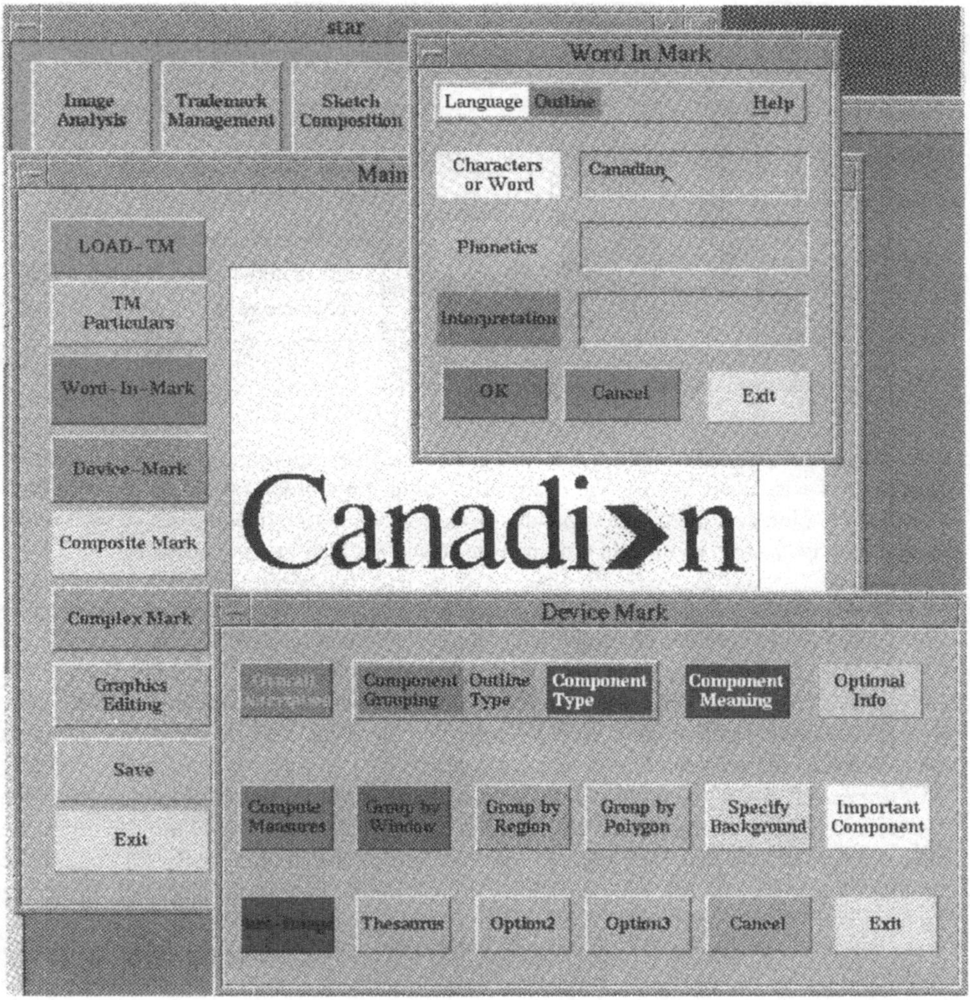


*Figure 3.* Segmentation of trademark images.

### *3.1. Color segmentation*

In color trademark images, the components of device mark are in different colors. Color segmentation is the only way to segment components of device mark. Color segmentation partitions 3-D color space. It is referred to as color coding [17] and extensively used in printing industry. A block diagram of color segmentation is shown in figure 4. The input color trademark images are represented as RGB primary colors images. The statistics of the image data in 3-D color space are then calculated. A sophisticated clustering algorithm in color space has been designed to find right color classes. Distance measures in classification

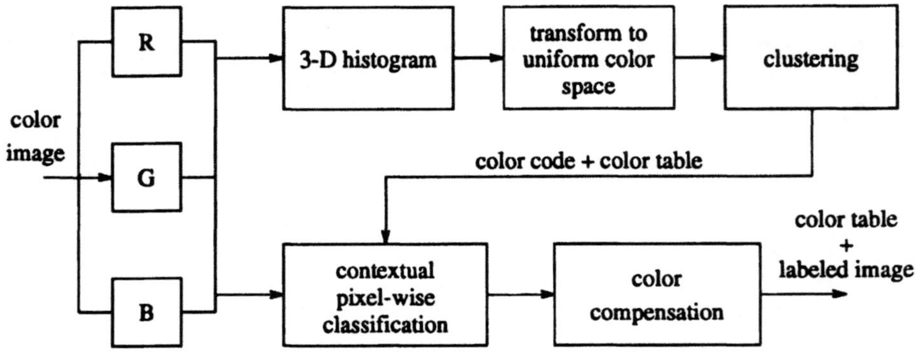


*Figure 4.* Block schematic of color segmentation.

are computed in the uniform color space to guarantee visual quality of segmented images. During pixel-wise classification we designed an algorithm which takes into account both cluster population and image data spatial correlation, so as to reduce noises in segmented images. Compensation of illuminating non-uniformity is also in consideration.

***3.1.1. Clustering in 3-D color space.*** Color image pixels can be regarded as points in a 3-D color space. As the number of components of a device mark is small and each component is represented by one color, and the optical reflection characteristics of each component tends to be consistent. Thus, the color of each component appears as one cluster in the color space. Color segmentation is used to first find out these clusters and then to assign a code to each of these clusters.

Unfortunately, for a given set of color images, there is not enough information about the number and population of clusters and, training data is usually not available. Therefore, we make the assumption that each color cluster has normal distribution with one peak value and there is a sufficient distance between every two color clusters. In this case, clustering can be simplified as a method for finding peaks and estimating distribution parameters.

The distance measure is of importance in clustering. The measure should be consistent with the visual resolution and should also be uniform in all directions in the entire color space. We used CIE 1976 uniform color system ($L^*$, $u^*$, $v^*$). The distance (color difference) can be calculated by an Euclidian distance:

$$d(L^*, u^*, v^*) = [\Delta L^* + \Delta u^* + \Delta v^*]^2 \qquad (1)$$

***3.1.2. The color code assignment of image data.*** To assign each pixel of image with color code is to classify the pixels one by one. We will describe in detail two major problems in reducing the classification error: design of classification method, and utilization of spatial information.

***3.1.3. Design of classification method.*** We have obtained the number of classes, the coordinates of center of each class, and corresponding amplitude value through cluster analysis in color space. Bays classifier is not applicable because the covariance matrices are not available. We can use minimum distance classifier. Minimum distance classifier makes implicit assumption that all classes have the same population. It is very often that within an image difference of number of pixels for colors is quite large. In this case, minimum distance classifier will result in large classification errors. Hence, we use a classifier which takes account of population differences in the color space. Suppose we have $N$ samples to classify into $M$ clusters: $\omega_1, \omega_2, \ldots,$ each cluster is Gaussian distributed $N(m_i, \sigma_i)$, contains $N_i$ samples. All clusters have the same covariance matrix. With the assumption $N_i \gg 1$, we have the optimal decision rule:

$$d(\mathbf{x}, \mathbf{m}_j) - 2\log[p(\omega_j)] = \min_i\{d(\mathbf{x}, \mathbf{m}_i) - 2\log[p(\omega_i)]\} \tag{2}$$

where $d()$ is the Euclidian distance from the sample to the center of class $\omega_i$ calculated in the uniform color space. The ratio of the population of class $\omega_i$ to the total samples, $N_i/N$ can be calculated by the ratio of corresponding amplitude value to the total values obtained by clustering in 3-D color space.

***3.1.4. Use of spatial correlation information.*** There have been some research attempt to improve the image classification accuracy through the use of spatial information (Young and Fu, 1986). These methods fall into three main categories: (1) relaxation method, which represents spatial correlation information by consistency coefficients, (2) contextual classifier, which directly makes use of spatial information, (3) use of image texture measure, together with spectrum data. The first two methods are very complicated and computationally expensive. The third method does not seem to be applicable in our case. We proposed to use a so-called predictive classifier based on the Markov field model of image data. In the first order Markov field, a pixel is closely related to its two neighbors (top and left) or four neighbors (top, down, left and right). It means the probability that a pixel and its four direct neighbors belong to the same class is relatively high. The following decision procedure is then applicable:

Perform classification using Eq. (2) in a raster scanning manner. For the current pixel

- Record the class label of top and left neighbor pixels $\omega_u$ and $\omega_l$ and corresponding distance measures $d_u()$ and $d_l()$.
- Calculate the decision function $d_c()$ which measures the similarity between the present pixel and class $\omega_u$, if $|d_u - d_c| < \theta$ then the pixel is assigned class $\omega_u$, otherwise, class $\omega_l$ is given the same consideration. If the pixel can not be classified to either class $\omega_u$ or class $\omega_l$, it will be classified using Eq. (2).

This method makes use of spatial correlation property of image data. It reduces noise in color coded images and saves considerable computation time.

## 4. Capturing visual features of trademark images

There are some work on shape description of trademark images. For example, Cortelazzo et al. used hierarchical contour coding [6]. The problem with this technique is the complexity in the retrieval of very large amount of trademarks.

Some trademark images are structured patterns. There are two issues in describing these visual patterns. One is the the structural feature—how the trademark image is composed by components. The other is shape/complexity measure of individual components.

### *4.1. Structural description*

Traditionally, structural features are represented by semantic networks or other tree/network data structures such as the one in [6]. To simplify the searching effort, we designed a flat representation by specifying the outline and component grouping types. By studying visual characteristics of trademark images, we have observed:

- Overall shape is more important than detailed structures. We choose to describe overall shape, individual components, and how components constitute the whole image.
- Many trademark images have outline/background, but the outline/background are not as important as the inside contents. Less importance is assigned to it.
- Components grouping has limited number of types. The type assignment is interactively done by the user.

Figure 5 shows a few types of outline/background (in the first row) and a few types of component grouping (in the second row) of trademark images.

### *4.2. Feature measures*

To characterize the visual features of the overall shape and individual component of trademark images, we have studied several feature extraction methods. We found that each

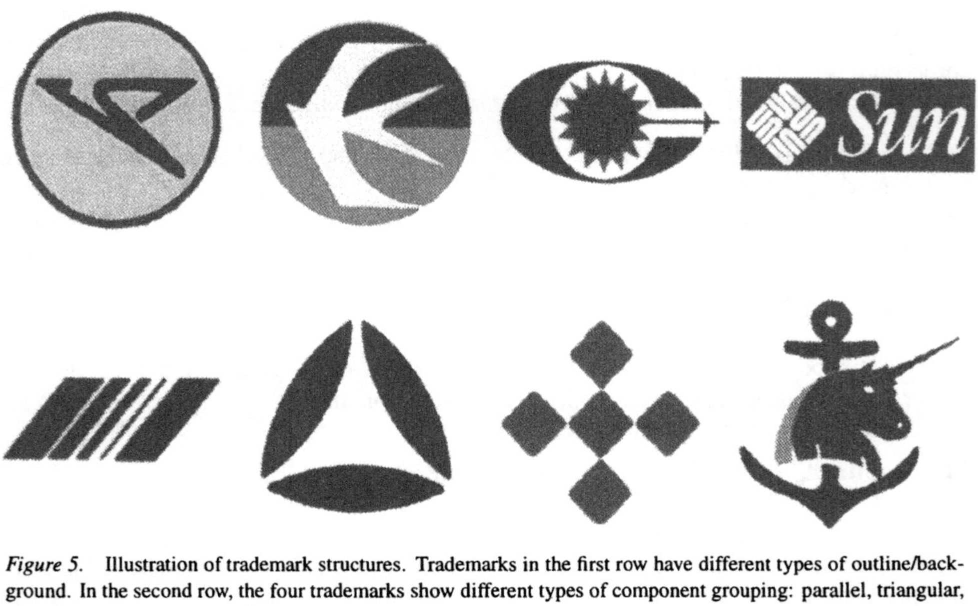


*Figure 5.* Illustration of trademark structures. Trademarks in the first row have different types of outline/background. In the second row, the four trademarks show different types of component grouping: parallel, triangular, star, and intersection respectively.

feature extraction method, either for shape, structure or texture, only captures one aspect of the visual pattern. Therefore, we have extracted three feature measures of the trademark images and fuse them together to characterize diverse and complex trademark images. These three feature measures are: Fourier descriptor of the shape, moment invariants, and projections. Fourier descriptor captures the outline shape, moment invariants represent the symmetry property, and projections describe the internal structure of the trademark images. Combination of these three feature measures will give a good description of visual features of trademark images.

***4.2.1. Fourier descriptor.*** Fourier descriptor for shape description was first proposed by Ali and Pavlidis [1], and more sophisticated method is reported in [2]. A brief description of the algorithms is as follows.

First, the contour of the trademark image is found after morphological filtering, then accumulated angular function of the contour is computed. Assume that the curve under consideration occupies $m$ pixels $V_0 \cdots V_{m-1}$. The starting point $V_0$ is selected and we define the change in angular direction at pixel $V_k$ as $\Delta\phi_k$. As contours are represented as 2-dimensional arrays in a square grid coordinate system, the direction of the line segment between any two neighboring pixels, $\Delta\phi_k$, is in multiples of $\pi/4$. The cumulative amount of angular bend between the starting point $V_0$ and point $V_k$ is defined as

$$\phi_k = \sum_{i=0}^{k} \Delta\phi_i \qquad 0 \leq k \leq m-1 \tag{3}$$

The Fourier coefficients $c_k$ is computed by the following Discrete Fourier transform equation:

$$c_k = \frac{1}{N} \sum_j \phi_j e^{-2\pi ijk/N} \tag{4}$$

In the Fourier transform domain, only the amplitudes are used as the feature measure. Since Fourier descriptors are derived by using the cumulative angular change in the contour, it is clear that these values only represent the topology of the contour and they contain no information relating to the absolute position or notational orientation of the trademark image. Therefore, the Fourier descriptors generated are invariant under translation and rotation. It is not sensitive to the starting point because of periodicity of Fourier transform.

***4.2.2. Moment invariants.*** Consider an image as a 2-D object in the space with grey level function as density function, $f(x, y)$, we define the $pq$'th moments as

$$m^{pq} = \sum_x \sum_y x^p y^q f(x, y) \tag{5}$$

The *Normalized Central Moments* to measure symmetry property of the objects can be derived accordingly:

$$\eta_{pq} = \sum_x \sum_y (x - \bar{x})^p (y - \bar{y})^q f(x, y) \tag{6}$$

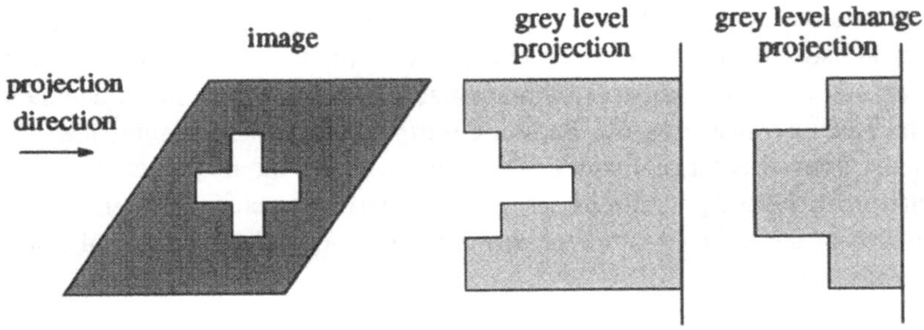


*Figure 6.* X-projection of grey level and grey level changes of images.

where $\bar{x} = \frac{m_{10}}{m_{00}}$, $\bar{y} = \frac{m_{01}}{m_{00}}$. From the second and third moments, a set of seven *invariant moments* are computed as follows:

$$\begin{aligned}
\phi_1 &= \eta_{20} + \eta_{02} \qquad (7)\\
\phi_2 &= (\eta_{20} - \eta_{02})^2 + 4\eta_{11}^2\\
\phi_3 &= (\eta_{30} - \eta_{02})^2 + (3\eta_{21} - \eta_{03})^2\\
\phi_4 &= (\eta_{30} + \eta_{12})^2 + (3\eta_{21} + \eta_{03})^2\\
\phi_5 &= (\eta_{30} - 3\eta_{12})(\eta_{30} + \eta_{12})[(\eta_{30} + \eta_{12})^2 - 3(\eta_{21} + \eta_{03})^2]\\
&\quad + (3\eta_{21} - \eta_{03})(\eta_{21} + \eta_{03})[3(\eta_{30} + \eta_{12})^2 - (\eta_{21} + \eta_{03})^2]\\
\phi_6 &= (\eta_{20} - \eta_{02})[(\eta_{30} + \eta_{12})^2 - (\eta_{21} + \eta_{03})^2]\\
&\quad + 4\eta_{11}(\eta_{30} + \eta_{12})(\eta_{21} + \eta_{03})\\
\phi_7 &= (3\eta_{21} - \eta_{03})(\eta_{30} + \eta_{12})[(\eta_{30} + \eta_{12})^2 - 3(\eta_{21} - \eta_{30})^2]\\
&\quad + [(3\eta_{12} - \eta_{30})(\eta_{21} + \eta_{03})[3(\eta_{30} + \eta_{12})^2 - (\eta_{21} + \eta_{03})^2]
\end{aligned}$$

This set of moments has been shown to be invariant to translation, rotation, and scale change.

***4.2.3. Projections.*** There are two types of projections: grey level projection and grey level change projection. The grey level projection is illustrated in figure 6. In the 2-D grid coordinate system, the X-projection of grey level is defined as the number of black pixels alone horizontal projection lines while the X-projection of grey level change projection is defined as the number of grey level changes alone horizontal projection lines. Projections capture certain internal structural properties of the images which Fourier descriptor and moment invariants do not.

### 4.3. *Match shape interpretation using fuzzy thesaurus*

Device mark meaning are conceptually defined words or phrases. To reduce description diversity, we adopted Vienna classification [11] which describes trademarks into a hierarchy of category, division and section. A fuzzy thesaurus was built to evaluate the similarity

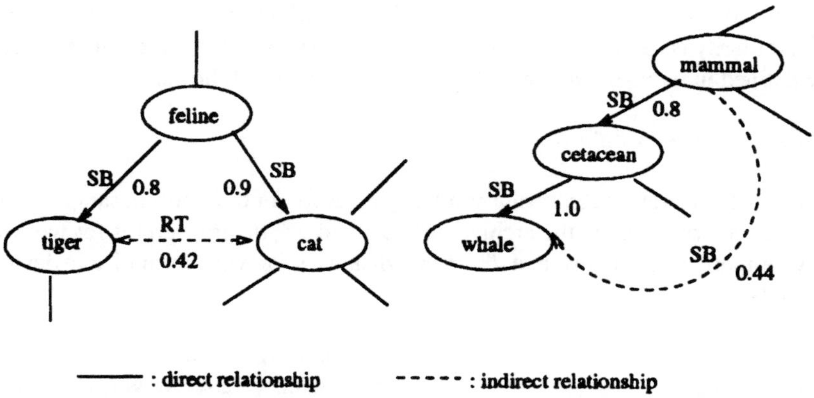


*Figure 7.* Examples of querying indirect relationship terms.

between sections of Vienna classifications, using a fuzzy multi-linkage thesaurus builder developed by Gao et al. [7].

In a thesaurus, a term represents a concept, which may be related to other concepts with many-to-many relationships. It is designed to include three types of thesaural relationships, they are equivalence, hierarchical, and associative. The equivalence relationship indicates that the terms are considered synonymous or quasi synonymous. The hierarchical relationship indicates the generic relationship between terms that are broader and narrower in concept. The associative relationship is found between terms which are closely related conceptually but are neither hierarchical nor equivalence relations. We implement these three types of relationships into six classes of detailed relationships: synonymous, related, sub-class, super-class, part-of and user-defined relationship. The user-defined relationship extends the flexibility of the thesaurus builder, by allowing users to define any desired type of relationship. The relationships among concepts are usually imprecise. We assign each thesaural relationship with a fuzzy factor to describe the degree of (strength of) relationship. Semantics-wise, the fuzzy factor represents the concepts of "very", "fairly", "slightly" and "rarely", etc.

The thesaurus builder's structure is like a semantic network. Each term is multi-linked with other terms. Term relationships are reciprocal, when one side of a relationship has been supplied the system should automatically provide the other side. It is the same when a relationship between two terms is deleted. In query processing, the fuzzy factor is used to rank the candidates.

Users can also use fuzzy reasoning to expand the searching range and retrieve more terms which have no direct relationship with the query term as shown in figure 7.

## 5. Composite similarity measures

Images usually have structured contents. Each of the components in the contents may have different features and can be measured using different features. This has been very well demonstrated by trademarks. The similarity among trademarks should take account of all aspects of word-in-mark and device mark. The contribution of individual aspects to the overall similarity is balanced by weights. The composite similarity measure for trademarks can be defined in terms of weighted distance and written as follows:

$$d_{cj} = w^w d^w_{ci} + w^d d^d_{cj} \tag{8}$$

where $d_{cj}$ is the overall or composite similarity measure for the "current sample" trademark and $j$th trademark image in the archive, $w^w$, $w^d$ and $d^w$, $d^d$ are weights for word-in-mark and device-mark, respectively, and $d^w$, $d^d$ are distances for word-in-mark and device-mark, respectively.

$$d^w_{cj} = \begin{cases} 0 & \text{if } \mathrm{wim}_c = \mathrm{wim}_j = \text{false} \\ \theta_w & \text{either } \mathrm{wim}_c = \text{false}, \text{ or } \mathrm{wim}_j = \text{false} \\ w^w_w d^w_{wcj} + w^w_p d^w_{pcj} + w^w_i d^w_{icj} & \text{if } \mathrm{wim}_c = \mathrm{wim}_j = \text{true} \end{cases}$$

where $\mathrm{wim}_c$, and $\mathrm{wim}_j$ are boolean functions to represent the presence or absence of word-in-mark in the current or $j$th trademark respectively, $w^w_w$, $w^w_p$, $w^w_i$ and $d^w_{wcj}$, $d^w_{pcj}$, $d^w_{icj}$ are weights and distances of words, phonetics, and interpretation for the current trademark and the $j$th trademark, respectively. $\theta_w$ is the penalty when one trademark has a word-in-mark but the other does not.

Similarly, the similarity for device mark is defined as

$$d^d_{cj} = \begin{cases} 0 & \text{if } \mathrm{dev}_c = \mathrm{dev}_j = \text{false} \\ \theta_d & \text{either } \mathrm{dev}_c = \text{false}, \text{ or } \mathrm{dev}_j = \text{false} \\ \frac{1}{N_{\text{comp}}} \sum_k \left( w^d_m d^d_{mkcj} + w^d_p d^d_{pkcj} + w^d_g d^d_{gkcj} \right) & \text{if } \mathrm{dev}_c = dev_j = \text{true} \end{cases}$$

where $\mathrm{dev}_c$ and $\mathrm{dev}_j$ are boolean functions to represent the presence or absence of device mark in the current or $j$th trademark respectively, $\theta_d$ is the penalty when one trademark has a device mark but the other does not. $w^d_m$, $w^d_p$, $w^d_g$ are weights for the meaning, structure, and shape/texture aspects for the device mark and $d^d_{mkcj}$, $d^d_{pkcj}$, $d^d_{gkcj}$ are distances of the meaning, structure, and shape/texture aspects of $k$th component of the device mark of the sample trademark and a component of the device mark of the $j$th trademark. Notice that the graphics components of device mark do not have any particular ordering when they are segmented. Any graphics component in the sample trademark can match any graphics component in the $j$th trademark. The distance of the device mark is then defined as the minimum distance between these two device marks.

Notice also that graphics components are not necessarily treated equally. For example, in the trademark image (3,3), the leaf graphic part is more important than the circle. Therefore, we distinguish such component as *major component*. If the major component of the device mark of the current trademark matches the major component of the device mark of the $j$th trademark, more weight should be put to such a distance than the distances of the other components.

$$d^d_{cj} = (1 - w_{\text{imp}}) \left( d^d_{cj} - \frac{1}{N_{\text{comp}}} d^d_{\text{imp-}cj} \right) + w_{\text{imp}} d^d_{\text{imp-}cj} \tag{9}$$

where $w_{\text{imp}}$ and $d^d_{\text{imp-}cj}$ are the weight factor and the distance for the major component.

*Table 1.* Similarity values for a set of word-pairs.

| $\text{Word}_1$ | $\text{Word}_2$ | $\text{Sim}_w$ | $\text{Sim}_p$ |
|---|---|---|---|
| asi | asea | 0.750000 | 0.333333 |
| foral | feral | 0.975000 | 0.975000 |
| cosmic | coshmick | 0.937500 | 0.979167 |
| armor | amor | 0.975000 | 0.800000 |
| creeza | kreeza | 0.916667 | 1.000000 |
| heart | hart | 0.975000 | 0.968750 |
| chikngrillas | chickutay | 0.854167 | 0.825000 |
| aero | aeron | 0.975000 | 0.750000 |
| gaynor | caynore | 0.857143 | 0.833333 |
| communication | com*tion | 0.942308 | 0.932692 |
| 3M | Three M | 0.142857 | 1.000000 |
| Fujitsu | Kodar | 0.000000 | 0.000000 |

We can adapt distance measure (in a broad sense) between device marks because the shape/texture measures are represented as vectors after feature extraction. Similarity measure for word-in-mark is measured by the number of the same ordered characters in the two words (Meadow, 1992). The formula is:

$$d_w^w = 1 - \text{sim}_w = 1 - \sum_k w_k l_k / l_{\text{word}} \tag{10}$$

where $s_w$ is the word similarity measure, $l_k, l_{\text{word}}$ are length of the $k$th common factor between two words and the length of the whole word. Several cases will be checked when actually computing the length of common factors. The word length is taken to be the average length of two words. Table 1 lists similarity measures between sets of two words, where $\text{sim}_w$, $\text{sim}_p$ are similarities for word and phonetics.

## 6. Evaluation and learning of similarity measures

Retrieval of conflicting trademarks of similar shape is referred to as content-based retrieval or feature-based retrieval. We have studied the evaluation of content-based retrieval and proposed a learning algorithm for similarity measures by fusing multiple feature measures [25]. This evaluation method has been applied to the shape retrieval of STAR to evaluate the shape retrieval engine and to tune the similarity functions. In this section, we will first describe the training and test data sets of 2D shapes, then explain the learning algorithm, and finally present the evaluation results.

### *6.1. Select of training and test data sets*

Evaluation of feature measures and similarity functions are application oriented. They must be done against a given set of objects—training data set. To define a training data set for content-based retrieval, let us define the ideal content-based retrieval first:

*Ideal content-based retrieval.* For any given sample, the retrieval result should exactly follow designer's expectation of similarity—all data items must be retrieved and be ordered from the most similar to the least similar.

Let us denote the training/test data set as:

$$d_1^s, d_{11}, d_{12}, \ldots; \; d_2^s, d_{21}, d_{22}, \ldots; \ldots$$

That means, when $d_1^s$ is used as a sample presented to the database $d_{11}, d_{12}, \ldots$ must be retrieved and ranked the same order in an ideal retrieval.

In reality, the retrieval result may be different from ideal one. We describe the difference by a rank list:

$$d_1^s\colon \; m_{11}, m_{12}, \ldots; \; d_2^s\colon \; m_{21}, m_{22}, \ldots; \ldots$$

where $m_{11}$ denotes the number of position difference of $d_{11}$ in the retrieval list. Assign unit loss to unit miss rank, the total loss is then the summation of all losses and normalized by the length of the testing data set $K$:

$$L = \frac{\sum_{ij} m_{ij}/K}{K} \tag{11}$$

We have designed two categories of training/test shapes: geometric shapes and trademark shapes. The variation of geometric shapes can be designed objectively. For example, one series of geometric shapes are regular polygens consisting of triangular, square, ..., until their extreme—circle. Geometric shapes are also designed to have variations on outline shape, interial structure, and symmetry.

Figure 10 shows a test data set of trademarks shapes. This was selected subjectively by voting among 10 people.

### 6.2. *Learning of similarity functions*

Figure 8 shows a network architecture for learning of similarity functions with fusion of these three shape feature measures, namely, fourier descriptors, moments, and projections. This network is a variation of multilayer feedforward network with back-propagation learning algorithm. Since our goal is to learn similarity functions between pairs of input patterns, we replace the input layer of ordinary feedforward network by comparison layer.

Overall speaking, the network consists of four layers: a data layer, a comparison layer, a hidden layer, and an output layer. The data layer has two arrays of network units: one sample data array and one data array. For a training data set $d_i^s, d_{i1}, d_{i2}, \ldots$, data pairs $(d_i^s, d_{i1}), (d_i^s, d_{i2}), \ldots$, are fed to the data layer sequentially, and in the output layer, unit number $1, 2, \ldots$, are expected to be active. That is to say that the activation of output units code the similarity of the input data pair.

In the comparison layer, there can be several arrays of units each representing one comparison method. Currently, we use two comparison methods: delta and normalized correlation. Comparison is made for every component of feature vectors.

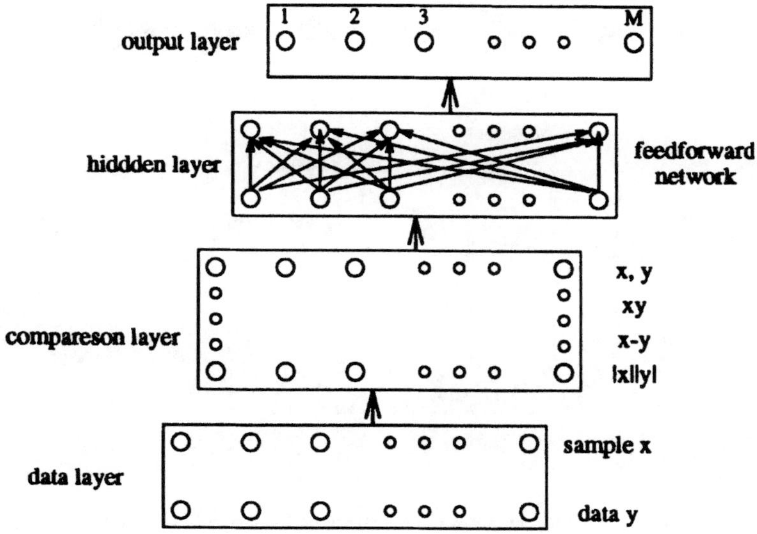


*Figure 8.* Neural networks for learning similarity functions and fusion of multiple feature measures.

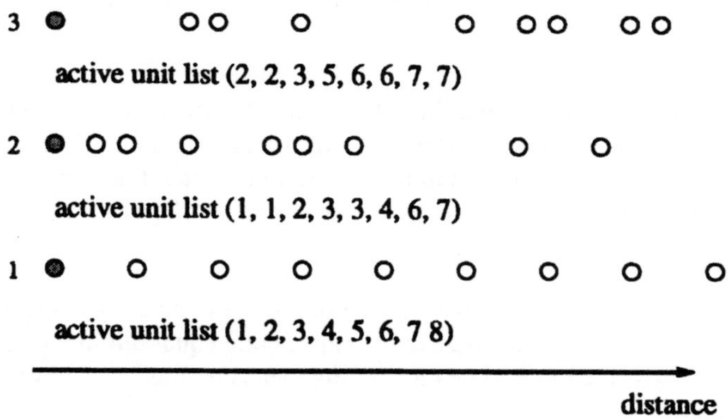


*Figure 9.* In the ranked lists of retrieval, the pair-wise distance may not be uniform. Here, filled circles represent sample data, and non-filled circles are data items in the ranked lists according to their similarity (here in the figure, the similarity is defined as distance) to the sample data. The first line is an ideal case where all pair-wise distances are the same. The second and third lines show differences.

The layers above the comparison layer constitute a feedforward network, which is designed to learn similarity function. The number of layers here determines the complexity of the similarity function. If we want the similarity function to be linear, two layers are adequate. Three or more layer network will be able to simulate any non-linear functions [18].

We must note that the distances/similarity between pairs of objects in the ranked lists are usually not equal, as illustrated in figure 9. In this case, it may not be true that the $j$th output unit becomes active when the sample data and the data item $d_{ij}$ is presented to the network.

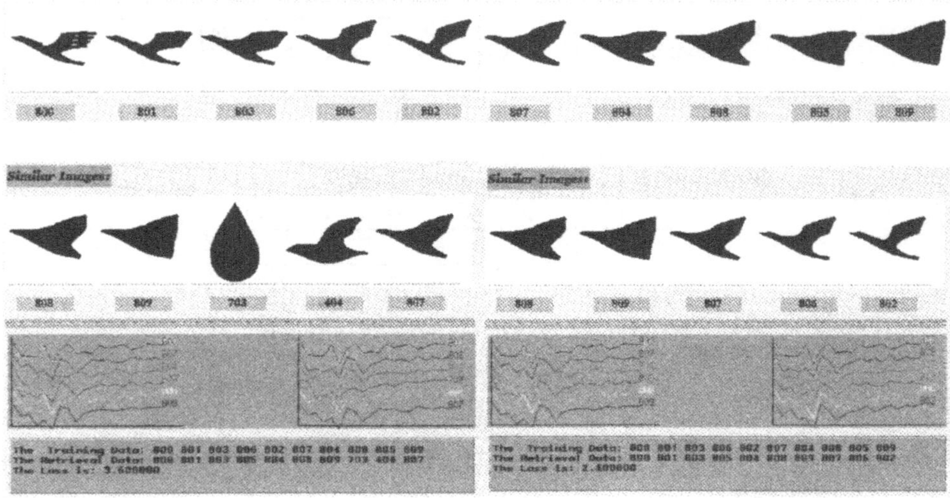

*Figure 10.* Above: a set of training data set—a sample trademark image followed by a set of similar trademark images arranged from the most similar to less similar. Below show the last 5 images of the two retrieval results. Curves are plot of shape feature measures of these images. On the left, without learning, there are unexpected images appear in the retrieval result, and image 806 and 802 never appear. On the right, after learning, the retrieval result is much more meaningful. The loss here (3.6 and 2.4) is scaled up by factor 10.

For example, the first output unit will be active when the first and the second data item are presented because both of them are very close to the sample data. To accommodate that, we can perform learning after all data items in a training data set have been presented. The training procedure is as follows:

1. Construct the network by letting the number of nodes of one array in the data layer equal feature measure size, and the number of output node equal number of elements in the ranked list. Choose the hidden layer according to the complexity you want the similarity function to have.
2. For one training data set, the sample data will remain attached to the sample data array, while other data items $d_{ij}$ in the training data set is fed to the data array one by one. Run the network for each data item, and record the activation of output units in a list.
3. The list of activation of output units is a queue containing the coding of similarities of the imput pairs $(d_i^s, d_{ij})$, $j = 1, 2, \ldots$. If the network is already properly trained, the similarity coding in the list should be in an incremental order. Calculate the error by finding the wrong order of those similarity codings. Back-propagate the error and modify the weights of the feedforward network.
4. Randomly apply training data sets to the network until all data sets have been applied.
5. Repeat this learning process until the network reaches certain stable state. If it converges, take these weights to formulate the similarity function. Otherwise, check the consistency of the training data.

### *6.3. Evaluating the shape retrieval*

After learning of similarity function for shape retrieval, an evaluation was conducted to test the effectiveness of the shape retrieval engine. The evaluation was carried out using the selected trademark shape test data set.

Figure 10 shows an example of the testing, which consists of several parts of screen dumps. The training data set contains several variations: first is the variation of detailed structure on the wing, and then followed by the angle between wing and body. The bird is finally transformed into a triangular like shape. Since the three shape measures are sensitive to angles, birds with large angle between wing and body (806, 802) were not retrieved for the retrieval engine using the composite similarity measure in Eq. (9), see the low-left part of figure 10, which shows the last five retrieved trademark images. Although image 703 and 404 are similar to the sample with respect to overall shape, they should not be ranked so high in the retrieval result from the point of view of trademark officers.

After learning, the retrieval engine has taken into account the factors of human interpretation which are represented in the training data set. Hence, the retrieval result on the low-right part of figure 10 is conceptually acceptable to trademark officers. This is well reflected by the loss of the retrieval: after learning, the loss is reduced to 0.24 from 0.36 (without learning).

## 7. Experimental results

Searching for the conflicting trademarks is carried out after presenting a completely segmented sample trademark. Indices are created for each graphic feature measures using the indexing method ContIndex described in [19]. It is used to narrow down candidate search space and reduce the searching time. This becomes effective and necessary when the database size is large. All possible candidates will be verified using the composite similarity measure discussed above.

Figure 11 shows a experimental result of searching using a sample trademark with device mark only as shown in the right display panel. The searched trademarks are ranked from the most similar to less similar. The first 9 trademarks are displayed on the 9 display areas in the order from top-left to bottom-right. By clicking on a display areas a corresponding trademark particulars and image will be displayed on the left. Activating button "more" to the left of 9 display areas will enable you to view more of searched trademarks.

Figure 12 shows searching results using word-in-mark. In (a), "ia" is the most similar one to "Canadian" because it is completely included in "Canadian". When phonetics is added to similarity measure, "ia" is no longer the most similar one—they do not have phonetics similarity since "ia" takes phonetics of two characters "i" and "a". (b) was obtained by using both words and phonetics.

The prototype STAR is implemented in unix work station using C programming language programming in an object-oriented manner. The first version of the prototype is tested against 3000 real trademarks collected from advertisements. Images are scanned in using color scanner and then normalized to a standard size of $400 \times 400$. Images are stored in the database using JPEK compression. After compression, each image is about 10–20 KB. A

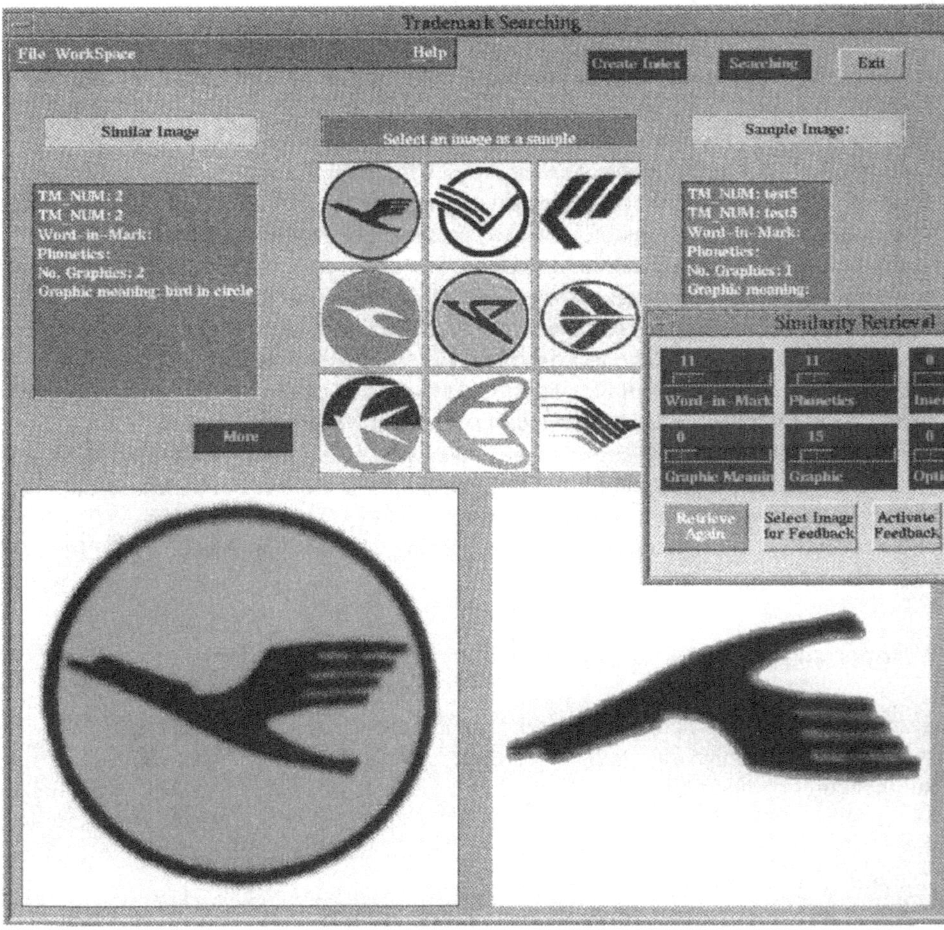


*Figure 11.* Sample search output for a device-mark as query trademark.

system of 10,000 trademarks will take 100–200 MB disk space. It is a reasonable storage requirement.

The system was tested against 500 trademarks given by a trademark office. The time taken to archive those given trademarks (3 days) and the retrieval results are all to their satisfactory: semi-automatic segmentation does take time in trademark archival phase, but it takes less time than manual filing of trademarks. STAR offers similarity retrieval capability which is very useful to guarantee the uniqueness of trademarks, but it is impossible when using manual filing. The average time for one retrieval of this trial system was around 5 second, including query processing, decoding and displaying trademark images.

Scaling up of the system is not a problem. There are three major components in query processing: matching word-in-mark, matching graphic meaning by fuzzy thesaurus based

(a) (b)

*Figure 12.* Trademark search output: (a) retrieval using words only. Among trademarks retrieved, "ia" is considered as the most similar because "ia" is wholly included in "Canadian". The words of all others partially match "Canadian", and therefore, ranked behind "ia". (b) Retrieval using words and phonetics. The words and phonetics have the same weights in the similarity measure. Among retrieved trademarks, "Canadian" and "Aerocancun" are considered the most similar because the common part "can" of both trademark words has the same pronunciation.

on vienna classification, and similarity searching of device marks. Vienna classification has limited vocabulary, increase of database size does not increase searching time. According to [19], the time needed to search the ContIndex of feature measures is proportional to the logarithm of the amount of trademarks in the database. We also use inverted file to index the word-in-mark, therefore, the searching time will not increase significantly when the database size increases. On the other hand, the retrieval time is nothing when it is compared with manual search. The time of manual search is in terms of hours.

## 8. Conclusions

We have presented a trademark archival and registration system STAR in this paper. It was developed using our content-based retrieval engine CORE. We have tackled difficult issues for conflict trademark retrieval, namely, searching multi-lingual word-in-mark and diverse trademark images, developed special similarity measures for word-in-mark, fuzzy thesarus to search trademark image by meaning match, and three feature extraction methods and learning method to fuse these feature measures for searching trademark images by shape. Our experimental results have shown the effectiveness of these techniques.

## References

1. F. Ali and T. Pavlidis, "Syntactic recognition of handwritten numerals," IEEE Trans. Syst. Man. Cybern., Vol. 7, pp. 537–541, 1977.

2. K. Arbter, W.E. Snyber, H. Burkhardt, and G. Hirzinger, "Application of affine-invariant Fourier descriptors recognition of 3-D objects," IEEE Trans. Pattern Anal. Machine Intell., Vol. 12, No. 7, 1990.
3. J. Bach, S. Paul, and R. Jain, "A visual information management system for the interactive retrieval of faces," IEEE Trans. on Knowledge and Data Engineering, Vol. 5, pp. 619–628, 1993.
4. P.B. Berra, C.Y.R. Chen, A. Ghafoor, C.C. Lin, T.D.C. Little, and D. Shin, "Architecture for distributed multimedia database systems," Computer Communications, Vol. 13, No. 4, pp. 217–231, May 1990.
5. S.K. Chang, C. Yan, D.C. Dimitroff, and T. Arndt, "An intelligent image database system," IEEE Trans. on Software Engineering, Vol. 14, pp. 681–688, 1988.
6. G. Cortelazzo, G.A. Mian, G. Vezzi, and P. Zamperoni, "Trademark shape description by string-matching techniques," Pattern Recognition, Vol. 27, No. 8, pp. 1005–1018, 1994.
7. Y.J. Gao, J.J. Lim, and A.D. Narasimhalu, "Fuzzy multilinkage thesaurus builder in multimedia information systems," The 3rd International Conference on Document Analysis and Recognition, Montreal, Canada, IEEE Computer Society, Aug. 1995.
8. W.I. Grosky, "Multimedia information systems," IEEE Multimedia, Spring, pp. 12–24, 1994.
9. W.I. Grosky and R. Mehrotra, "Index-based object recognition in poctorial data management," Computer Vision, Graphics, and Image Processing, Vol. 52, pp. 416–436, 1990.
10. K. Hornk, M. Stinchocombe, and H. White, "Multi-layer feedforward networks are universal approximators," Neural Networks, Vol. 2, pp. 359–366, 1989.
11. "International classification of the fifurative elements of marks," Vienna Agreement of June 12, 1973, World Intellectual Property Organization (WIPO), WIPO Publication No. 502(E), Geneva, 1993.
12. T. Kato, "Database architecture for content-based image retrieval," SPIE Image Storage and Retrieval Systems, Vol. 1662, pp. 112–122, 1992.
13. A. Pentland, R.W. Picard, and S. Sclaroff, "Photobook: Tools for content based manipulation of image databases," SPIE Conf. Storage and Retrieval of Image and Video Databases II, No. 2185, Feb. 6–10, 1994.
14. E. Petrakis and S. Orphanoudakis, "Methodology for the representation, indexing and retrieval of images by content," Image and Vision Computing, Vol. 11, pp. 504–520, 1993.
15. S.W. Smoliar and H.J. Zhang, "Content-based video indexing and retrieval," IEEE MultiMedia, Summer, pp. 62–72, 1994.
16. A. Tversky, "Features of similarity," Psychological Review, Vol. 84, pp. 327–352, 1977.
17. J.K. Wu, "Color coding of images," Journal of Signal Processing of China, Vol. 5, pp. 1–6, 1986.
18. J.K. Wu, *Neural Networks and Simulation*, Marcel Dekker, Inc., New York, 1994.
19. J.K. Wu, "Content-based indexing of multimedia databases," IEEE Trans. KDE, (to appear).
20. J.K. Wu and A.D. Narasimhalu, "Fuzzy content-based image databases," Information Processing and Management, (to appear).
21. J.K. Wu, F. Gao, and P. Yang, "Model-based 3-D object recognition," Proc. Second International Conference on Automation, Robotics and Computer Vision, Sept. 15–18, Singapore, 1992.
22. J.K. Wu, Y.H. Ang, C.P. Lam, H.H. Loh, and A. Desai Narasimhalu, "Inference and Retrieval of Facial Images," ACM Multimedia Journal, Vol. 2, No. 1, pp. 1–14, 1994.
23. J.K. Wu, B.M. Mehtre, Y.J. Gao, P.C. Lam, and A. Desai Narasimhalu, "STAR—A multimedia database system for trademark registration," Applications of Databases, Lecture Notes in Computer Science, Vol. 819, W. Litwin and T. Risch (Eds.), Proc. First International Conference, ADB-94, Vadstena, Sweden, June 1994, pp. 109–122, Springer-Verlag.
24. J.K. Wu, A.D. Narasimhalu, B.M. Mehtre, C.P. Lam, and Y.J. Gao, "CORE: A content-based retrieval engine for multimedia information systems," ACM Multimedia Systems, Vol. 3, pp. 3–25, 1995.
25. J.K. Wu et al., "Evaluation of feature measures and similarity measures for content-based retrieval," SPIE Symposium on Digital Image Storage and Archiving Systems, Philadelphia, SPIE Proceedings, Vol. 2606, Oct. 25–26, 1995.
26. A. Yoshitaka, S. Kishida, M. Hirakawa, and T. Ichikawa, "Knowledge-assisted conetent-based retrieval for multimedia databases," Proc. International Conf. on Multimedia Computing and Systems, Boston, Massachusetts, May 14–19, 1994, pp. 131–139.
27. A. Zink and C.C. Jaffe, "Medical imaging databases," Investigative Radiology, Vol. 28, pp. 366–372, 1993.

**Jian-Kang Wu** received his Bachelor degree from the University of Science and Technology of China, and Ph.D. from the University of Tokyo. He is now with the Institute of Systems Science (ISS), National University of Singapore, heading a team for the research on active media computing.

Prior to join ISS, he worked in the University of Science and Technology of China as a full Professor until 1992. He also worked as an Alexander-Humboldt research fellow in University of Erlangen-Nunberg in 1989, visiting associate professor in University of Pittsburgh in 1986, foreign research fellow in University of Tokyo in 1982, academic visitor in Imperial College London in 1980. His research interests are active media computing, image information systems, geographic information systems, computer vision and neural networks.

Dr. Wu is an author of 4 books and more than 50 journal papers. He have conducted more than 15 projects. He awarded a title "Research Pioneer" from National Committee of Science and National Committee of Education of China, and prizes from Chinese Academy of Science.

**Chian-Prong Lam** is born in 1964 in Singapore. He received his B.Eng. Honours from the National University of Singapore in 1989. He was awarded a research scholarship from the same university to work on a non-contact high resolution 3-D profilometry system for generating the profiles of lenses. He received his M.Eng. in 1992.

He is currently a senior research engineer in the Institute of Systems Science conducting research in graphics manipulation, image processing and image understanding. His research interest is in image understanding and image databases.

**Babu M. Mehtre** is a researcher with the archival and retrieval of multimedia information group at ISS. He got his B.E. (Electronics and Communications Engineering) with distinction from Gulbarga University in 1983, M.Tech.

(Automation and Control Eng'g), and Ph.D. (Engineering) from Indian Institute of Technology, Kharagpur, in 1984 and 1990 respectively.

Dr. Mehtre was with the Image Processing Group at CMC R&D Centre, Hyderabad, India, from 1985 to 1992. During this time, he worked on a fingerprint identification system project and a map understanding system. He has received four national awards from the Government of India for his work in fingerprints. He has also received a special award for his Master's thesis. He was a visiting scholar at the Pattern Recognition and Image Processing Lab, Michigan State University during the first quarter of 1990.

Dr. Mehtre has reviewed papers for various international journals and conferences, and is on the program committee of the International Workshop on Graphics Recognition (GREC'95), Pennsylvania State University, August 1995. He is a member of IEEE, Pattern Recognition Society, and Singapore Computer Society. His areas of interests include graphics, image processing, pattern recognition, multimedia systems, and applications.

**Yong Jian Gao** received his B.Eng. and M.Eng. degrees from the Department of Electronic Engineering of the University of Science and Technology of China in 1987 and 1990 respectively. He is a research engineer in the Institute of Systems Science. His research interests include multimedia information retrieval and signal processing.

**Arcot Desai Narasimhalu** is an associate director at the Institute of Systems Science, National University of Singapore.

Dr. Narasimhalu is a member of the editorial boards of Pergamon's Press' Expert Systems with Applications, Information Processing and Management, British Computer Society's Computer Journal, ACM/Springer Verlag's Journal on Multimedia Systems and Singapore Computer Society's Journal on Information Technology. He has been the Program chair, Co-chair, Regional chair, and member of program committees of several regional and international conferences. He has also been the organizing chairperson for some conferences. He has published several technical papers in journals, books and conference proceedings. He has coedited Pergamon Press' book on "The Operational Expert Systems in the Far-east Asia". He has been mentioned in the recent "Who is Who in the World". He has been a consultant to several organizations and regularly reviews papers for some of the IEEE and ACM journals. Several research prototypes developed under his direction have been transferred as products.

Dr. Narasimhalu's present interests include System security, Mobile computing, Multimedia Systems, Expert Systems, Heterogeneous database management, and Decision Support Systems.

Dr. Narasimhalu has a Ph.D. in Electrical Engineering from the University of Hawaii. He had earlier earned a Masters of Technology degree in Electrical Engineering (light current) from the Indian Institute of Technology, Madras and Bachelor of Engineering degree in Electronics and Communications from the Madras University.

Dr. Narasimhalu worked with the R&D Labs of the Indian Telephone Industries from 1974 to 1980, was a visiting scientist with IBM Japan from 1984 to 1985 and has been with the Institute of Systems Science since 1985. He has about 20 years of cumulative research experience.

GPSR Compliance

*The European Union's (EU) General Product Safety Regulation (GPSR) is a set of rules that requires consumer products to be safe and our obligations to ensure this.*

*If you have any concerns about our products, you can contact us on ProductSafety@springernature.com*

In case Publisher is established outside the EU, the EU authorized representative is:

Springer Nature Customer Service Center GmbH
Europaplatz 3
69115 Heidelberg, Germany

**Batch number: 10620141**

Printed by Printforce, the Netherlands